# 7th

# Science

## Daily Practice Workbook
### 20 weeks of fun activities

ARGOPREP

$HO^2$ $NO^2$

$CH$

**Physical Science** • **Life Science** • **Earth & Space Science**

ArgoPrep is one of the leading providers of supplemental educational products and services. We offer affordable and effective test prep solutions to educators, parents and students. Learning should be fun and easy! To access more resources visit us at www.argoprep.com.

Our goal is to make your life easier, so let us know how we can help you by e-mailing us at: info@argoprep.com.

- ArgoPrep is a recipient of the prestigious **Mom's Choice Award**.

- ArgoPrep also received the 2019 **Seal of Approval** from Homeschool.com for our award-winning workbooks.

- ArgoPrep was awarded the 2019 **National Parenting Products Award**, **Gold Medal Parent's Choice Award** and **the Tillywig Brain Child Award**.

## SCIENCE SERIES

Science Daily Practice Workbook by ArgoPrep is an award-winning series created by certified science teachers to help build mastery of foundational science skills. Our workbooks explore science topics in depth with ArgoPrep's 5 E'S to build science mastery: Engaging, Exploring, Explaining, Experimenting, and Elaborating. All of our curriculum is aligned with the latest Next Generation Science Standards.

# Introduction

**Welcome to our 7th grade science workbook!**

This workbook has been specifically designed to help students build mastery of foundational science skills that are taught in seventh grade. This workbook provides a comprehensive twenty weeks of instruction through multiple different branches of science. Students will start with physical science and chemistry. It then covers Earth science followed by Space science. The last topics focus on human impacts on the environment.

This workbook takes a micro to macro approach of science. At the start, students learn how atoms make up everything. In weeks 1-5, the activities cover atomic composition, chemical reactions, and thermal energy. Then, students learn about how the Earth cycles different materials and about populations and ecology.

In weeks 6-11, cycling of matter, photosynthesis, and ecosystem biodiversity are covered. On a larger scale, students learn about how the Earth has changed over time and what resources are present due to those changes. In weeks 12-20, the geologic timescale, Earth's resources, and how humans are impacting those resources are covered.

The activities end with what students can do to have a better impact on the Earth. This small to large progression of science in the world is helpful in building and organizing knowledge as students learn about the different topics.

# Table of Contents

# How to Use the Book

This workbook is specifically geared toward seventh grade students & teachers. This book provides twenty weeks of material. Each week is broken down into an engagement section with a short reading and questions, an exploration activity, an opportunity for students to explain their understanding, an experiment, and an opportunity for students to elaborate on what they know.

By exploring a topic through hands-on activities, concepts are made clear in a logical progression. Each week focuses on one specific topic within the section. More information about the weekly structure can be found in the Weekly Planner section.

Teachers may use this book for the Next Generation Science Standards curriculum for seventh grade. This content could also be used in grades 6-8 if lessons are taught in a different order, as the standards fit the grade band of grades 6-8.

Some lessons or activities take longer than others, based on the type of material covered. Many of the activity days could take place in half an hour or less, and you can have students work independently or collaboratively.

## How to access video explanations?

Go to **argoprep.com/science7**
OR scan the QR Code:

## Weekly Planner

| Day | Activity | Description |
|---|---|---|
| 1 | Engaging with the Topic | Read a short text on the topic and answer multiple choice questions. |
| 2 | Exploring the Topic | Interact with the topic on a deeper level by collecting, analyzing and interpreting data. |
| 3 | Explaining the Topic | Make sense of the topic by explaining and beginning to draw conclusions about the data. |
| 4 | Experimenting with the Topic | Investigate the topic through hands-on, easy to implement experiments. |
| 5 | Elaborating on the Topic | Reflect on the topic and use all information learned to draw conclusions and evaluate results. |

# List of Topics

| Unit | Week | Topic | Standard |
|---|---|---|---|
| Physical Science | 1 | Thermal Energy | MS-PS1-4 |
| Physical Science | 2 | Atomic Composition | MS-PS1-1 |
| Physical Science | 3 | Chemical Reaction | MS-PS1-2 |
| Physical Science | 4 | Conservation of Mass | MS-PS1-5 |
| Physical Science | 5 | Thermal Energy Test | MS-PS1-6 |
| Life Science | 6 | Photosynthesis | MS-LS1-6 |
| Life Science | 7 | Ecosystem Resources | MS-LS2-1 |
| Life Science | 8 | Organism Interactions | MS-LS2-2 |
| Life Science | 9 | Cycling of Matter | MS-LS2-3 |
| Life Science | 10 | Population Changes | MS-LS2-4 |
| Life Science | 11 | Maintaining Biodiversity | MS-LS2-5 |
| Earth & Space Science | 12 | Geologic Timescale | MS-ESS1-4 |
| Earth & Space Science | 13 | Geoscience Processes | MS-ESS2-2 |
| Earth & Space Science | 14 | Plate Tectonics | MS-ESS2-3 |
| Earth & Space Science | 15 | Cycling of Earth's Materials | MS-ESS2-1 |
| Earth & Space Science | 16 | Cycling of Water | MS-ESS2-4 |
| Earth & Space Science | 17 | Earth's Resources | MS-ESS3-1 |
| Earth & Space Science | 18 | Natural Hazards | MS-ESS3-2 |
| Earth & Space Science | 19 | Human Impact | MS-ESS3-3 |
| Earth & Space Science | 20 | Human Populations | MS-ESS3-4 |

## Next Generation Science Standards Correlation Guide

| Unit | Next Generation Science Standard | Topic | Description of Standard |
|---|---|---|---|
| Physical Science | 1 | MS-PS1-4 | Develop a model that predicts and describes changes in particle motion, temperature, and state of a pure substance when energy is added or removed. |
| Physical Science | 2 | MS-PS1-1 | Develop models to describe the atomic composition of simple molecules and extended structures. |
| Physical Science | 3 | MS-PS1-2 | Analyze and interpret data on the properties of substances before and after the substances interact to determine if a chemical reaction has occurred. |
| Physical Science | 4 | MS-PS1-5 | Develop and use a model to describe how the total number of atoms does not change in a chemical reaction and thus mass is conserved. |
| Physical Science | 5 | MS-PS1-6 | Undertake a design project to construct, test, and modify a device that either releases or absorbs thermal energy by chemical processes. |
| Life Science | 6 | MS-LS1-6 | Construct a scientific explanation based on evidence for the role of photosynthesis in the cycling of matter and flow of energy into and out of organisms. |
| Life Science | 7 | MS-LS2-1 | Analyze and interpret data to provide evidence for the effects of resource availability on organisms and populations of organisms in an ecosystem. |
| Life Science | 8 | MS-LS2-2 | Construct an explanation that predicts patterns of interactions among organisms across multiple ecosystems. |
| Life Science | 9 | MS-LS2-3 | Develop a model to describe the cycling of matter and flow of energy among living and nonliving parts of an ecosystem. |

| Unit | Next Generation Science Standard | Topic | Description of Standard |
|---|---|---|---|
| Life Science | 10 | MS-LS2-4 | Construct an argument supported by empirical evidence that changes to physical or biological components of an ecosystem affect populations. |
| Life Science | 11 | MS-LS2-5 | Evaluate competing design solutions for maintaining biodiversity and ecosystem services. |
| Earth & Space Science | 12 | MS-ESS1-4 | Construct a scientific explanation based on evidence from rock strata for how long the geologic time scale is used to organize Earth's 4.6-billion-year-old history. |
| Earth & Space Science | 13 | MS-ESS2-2 | Construct an explanation based on evidence for how geoscience processes have changed Earth's surface at varying time and spatial scales. |
| Earth & Space Science | 14 | MS-ESS2-3 | Analyze and interpret data on the distribution of fossils and rocks, continental shapes, and seafloor structures to provide evidence of the past plate motions. |
| Earth & Space Science | 15 | MS-ESS2-1 | Develop a model to describe the cycling of Earth's materials and the flow of energy that drives this process. |
| Earth & Space Science | 16 | MS-ESS2-4 | Develop a model to describe the cycling of water through Earth's systems driven by energy from the sun and the force of gravity. |
| Earth & Space Science | 17 | MS-ESS3-1 | Construct a scientific explanation based on evidence for how the uneven distributions of Earth's mineral, energy, and groundwater resources are the result of past and current geoscience processes. |
| Earth & Space Science | 18 | MS-ESS3-2 | Analyze and interpret data on natural hazards to forecast future catastrophic events and inform the development of technologies to mitigate their effects. |

| Unit | Next Generation Science Standard | Topic | Description of Standard |
|---|---|---|---|
| Earth & Space Science | 19 | MS-ESS3-3 | Apply scientific principles to design a method for monitoring and minimizing a human impact on the environment. |
| Earth & Space Science | 20 | MS-ESS3-4 | Construct an argument supported by evidence for how increases in human population and per-capita consumption of natural resources impact Earth's systems. |

# WEEK 1

# Physical Science
## Thermal Energy
MS-PS1-4

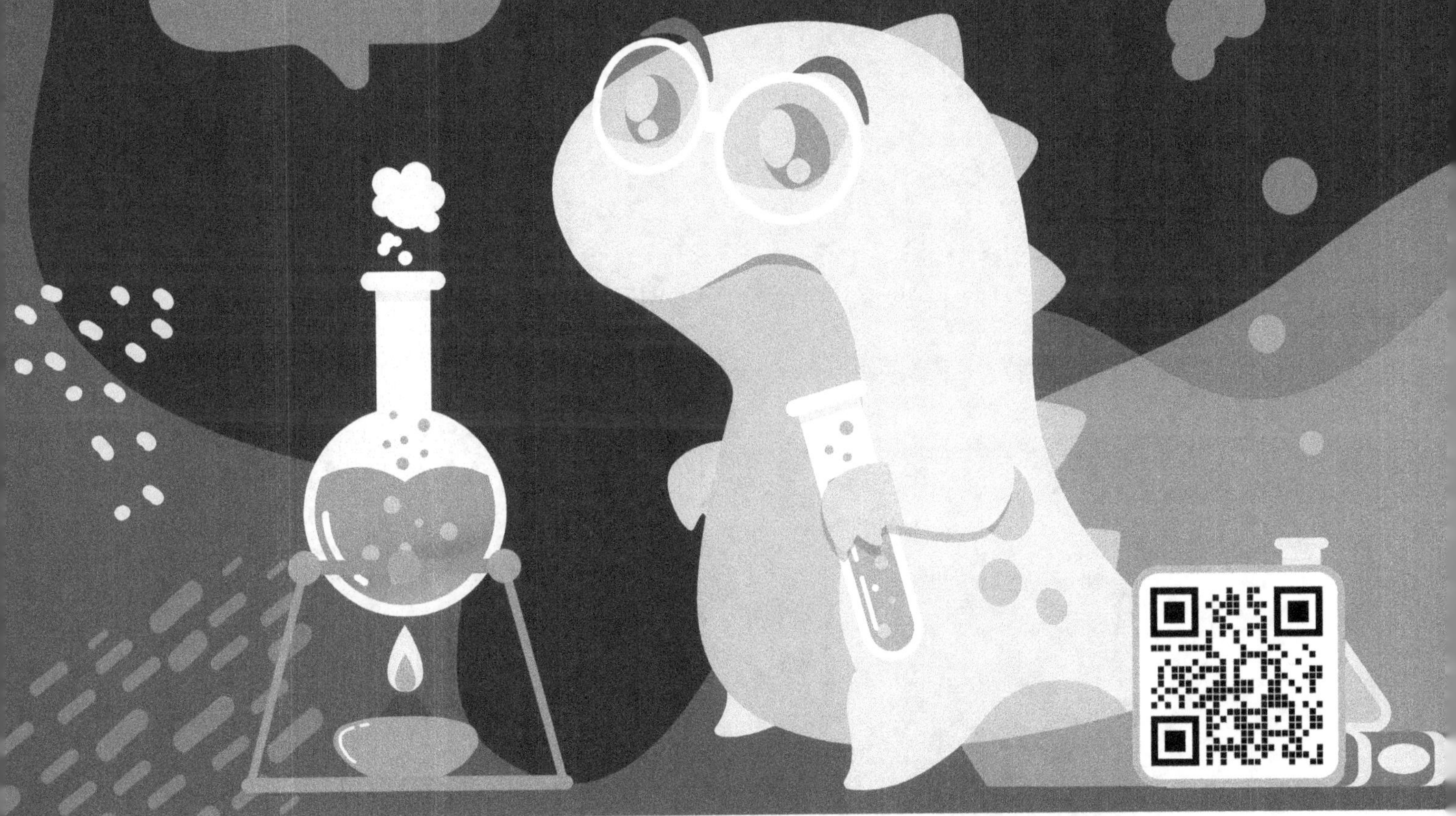

Develop a model that predict and describes changes in particle motion, temperature, and state of a pure substance when energy is added or removed.

**Directions:** Read the text below. Then answer the questions that follow.

## How Molecules Move

Matter is made up of molecules that are always in a state of motion. Molecules are always moving, if even by just a little bit. Molecules make up solids, liquids, and gases. In a solid, the molecules are close together and they barely move at all. In a liquid, the molecules are a medium distance apart and move a medium amount. In a gas, the molecules are far apart and move around quickly. The term for molecules vibrating at higher rates when the substance is warmer is called thermal energy. All matter has **thermal energy,** even if it feels cold.

1. Solids, liquids, and gases are made up of:

   **A.** Air

   **B.** Water

   **C.** Heat

   **D.** Molecules

2. Molecules in a solid move:

   **A.** Medium

   **B.** Fast

   **C.** Slow

   **D.** None of the above

3. _____ molecules move a medium amount.

   **A.** Liquid

   **B.** Gas

   **C.** Heat

   **D.** Solid

*Yesterday, you learned that molecules vibrate in increasing amounts when the temperature increases. Today, you will explore how these concepts work.*

**Directions:** Read each text below. Then answer the questions that follow.

## Solid Matter

Hold an ice cube in your hand. Notice what begins to happen to the ice cube.

1. Did you notice some of the ice was melting?

   **A.** Yes

   **B.** No

## Liquid Matter

Put a glass of water on the counter. Drop a single drop of food coloring into it. Over time, it will spread out and fill the container with color.

2. Did you see the color swirling around in the cup?

   **A.** Yes

   **B.** No

## Gas Matter

Have an adult boil a pot of water on the stove. When the water starts to boil (large, rolling bubbles), notice what begins to form over it. (**Warning: Adult supervision required)**

3. Did you see water vapor forming above the pot?

   **A.** Yes

   **B.** No

*Yesterday, you explored the concept of thermal energy in solids, liquids, and gases. Today, you will explain how this is possible.*

**Directions:** Read each text below. Then answer the questions that follow.

## Solid Matter

You discovered that your body heat will melt an ice cube.

1. Explain what you think is happening to the molecules as the ice melts.

## Liquid Matter

You discovered that color will disperse into a liquid without having to stir it.

2. Explain what you think is happening to the molecules inside of the liquid.

## Gas Matter

You discovered that boiling water will create water vapor, or steam.

3. Explain how you think the liquid turns into a gas.

*You have spent several days learning about thermal energy and how it works. Today, you will experiment with molecular motion.*

### Materials:

1. Three Cups
2. Very Cold Water
3. Room Temperature Water
4. Hot Water
5. Food Coloring (3 droppers, ideally the same color)
6. Timer

### Procedure:

1. Fill one cup with hot water, one with room temperature water, and one with cold water.
2. You may need a helper for this part. At the same time, drop a single drop of food coloring into each cup. Start the timer.
3. Record how long it takes for each color to disperse in each cup.
4. Record your answers for the questions below, repeating, as necessary.

### Follow-Up Questions:

1. Draw a picture of what is happening to the molecules inside the hot water cup.

2. Draw a picture of what is happening to the molecules inside the room temperature water cup.

3. Draw a picture of what is happening to the molecules inside the cold water cup.

4. What do you think would happen if you put food coloring on ice? Explain.

*Yesterday, you collected data while experimenting with food coloring and different temperatures of water. Today, you will use that data to draw conclusions about thermal energy.*

**Directions:** Read and answer each question below.

1. How fast did the food coloring spread out in the cold water?

2. How fast did the food coloring spread out in the hot water?

3. What can you conclude about the motion of the molecules?

4. The motion of the molecules in liquid is _____ compared to gases.

   **A.** faster

   **B.** medium

   **C.** slower

5. You know that solids, liquids and gases are made up of molecules. How are the molecules in these things different from each other?

6. Why do you think this?

# WEEK 2

# Physical Science
## Atomic Composition

MS-PS1-1

$C_6H_{12}O_6$

Develop models to describe the atomic composition of simple molecules and extended structures.

ARGOPREP

**Directions:** Read the text below. Then answer the questions that follow.

## Atoms Make up Everything

Everything, living or nonliving is made up of atoms. **Atoms** are tiny particles of pure elements, like you would see on the Periodic Table of the Elements. An **element** is a pure substance. A single carbon atom is one unit of carbon, and a single hydrogen atom is one unit of hydrogen. Atoms combine to form **molecules.** A water molecule is made up of two hydrogen, and one oxygen. A methane molecule is one carbon and four hydrogen.

1. What is the term for atoms combined together?

   **A.** Atoms

   **B.** Molecules

   **C.** Elements

   **D.** Chemical Reactions

2. What is the term for a pure substance?

   **A.** Atoms

   **B.** Molecules

   **C.** Elements

   **D.** Chemical Reactions

3. What is the term for the tiny particles which make up a pure substance?

   **A.** Atoms

   **B.** Molecules

   **C.** Elements

   **D.** Chemical Reactions

*Yesterday, you learned that atoms make up everything. Today we will explore how this works.*

**Directions:** Read each text below. Then answer the questions that follow.

## Atoms

Look around you. Everything is made up of atoms, including solids, liquids, and gases.

1.  Is it surprising that everything is made up of tiny particles?

    **A.** Yes

    **B.** No

## Elements

Look at a Periodic Table of Elements. Think of all of the elements that make up everything around you.

2.  Are there a large number of elements in the world?

    **A.** Yes

    **B.** No

## Molecules

Think of any molecules that you know of. For example, sugar is $C_6H_{12}O_6$.

3.  Are some molecules really complicated?

    **A.** Yes

    **B.** No

*Yesterday, you explored the concept of atoms making up molecules. Today, you will explain how this is possible.*

**Directions:** Read each text below. Then answer the questions that follow.

## Atoms

You discovered that atoms make up everything.

1. Explain how this is possible.

## Elements

You discovered that atoms are made up of different elements that can be found on the Periodic Table of the Elements.

2. Explain how elements come together to form molecules.

## Molecules

You discovered that molecules are made of single atoms of elements combined.

3. Explain what molecules are made of.

*You have spent several days learning about, exploring and explaining atomic composition. Today you will experiment with using atoms to build molecules.*

### Materials:

1. Beads of different colors

### Procedure:

1. Use a different colored bead to represent each of the following elements: carbon = pink, oxygen = blue, hydrogen = orange
2. Make a model of oxygen gas ($O_2$) by placing two blue beads next to each other.
3. Make a model of water by creating $H_2O$ by placing two hydrogen (orange) next to one oxygen (blue).
4. Make a model of sugar (also called glucose) by creating $C_6H_{12}O_6$.

### Follow-Up Questions:

1. Are all of the models you created molecules?

.................................................................................................................................

.................................................................................................................................

.................................................................................................................................

.................................................................................................................................

2. Which molecule is the most simple?

.................................................................................................................................

.................................................................................................................................

.................................................................................................................................

.................................................................................................................................

.................................................................................................................................

$O_2$

$H_2O$

$C_6H_{12}O_6$

3. Which molecule is most complex?

_____

_____

_____

_____

_____

4. In your opinion, are beads a good model of atoms?

_____

_____

_____

_____

_____

5. Why did you use three different colors of beads?

_____

_____

_____

_____

_____

_____

_____

*Yesterday, you collected data while experimenting with modeling different molecules. Today, you will use that data to draw conclusions about atoms and molecules.*

**Directions:** Read and answer each question below.

1. Do you interact with the molecules you created in your daily life?

   ................................................................

   ................................................................

2. Do beads serve as a good model of atoms and molecules?

   ................................................................

   ................................................................

3. Molecules are made up of atoms that are bonded together. What could you use to bond the beads together?

   ................................................................

   ................................................................

4. All atoms are made up of single:

   **A.** Elements          **C.** Molecules

   **B.** Patterns

5. Can you think of any other molecules that you interact with in your daily life?

   ................................................................

   ................................................................

6. Is there a better material we could model atoms with instead of beads?

   ................................................................

   ................................................................

# WEEK 3

# Physical Science
## Chemical Reaction

MS-PS1-2

$O^2$

$HO^2$   HCL

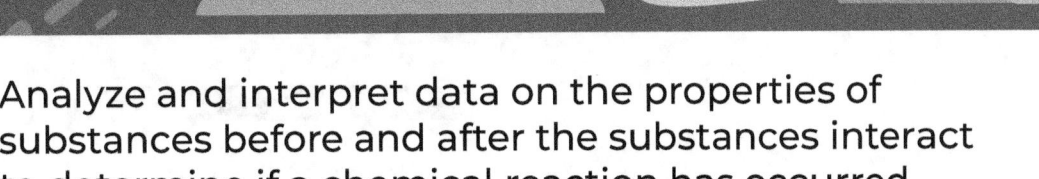

Analyze and interpret data on the properties of substances before and after the substances interact to determine if a chemical reaction has occurred.

ARGOPREP

**Directions:** Read the text below. Then answer the questions that follow.

## Chemical Reactions Everywhere

Chemical reactions take place all of the time in our daily lives. Everything from eating food, to cleaning the shower, to baking involves a chemical reaction. A chemical reaction is when multiple substances react to create a new substance. The substances that react together are called the **reactants,** because they do the reacting. A chemical reaction can be identified by things like a color change, production of a gas, flame, or odor. The substance that results from the chemical reaction is called the **product.**

1. What is NOT a sign of a chemical reaction?

   **A.** Odor

   **B.** Flame

   **C.** Color Change

   **D.** Freezing

2. The name of the starting substances is:

   **A.** Product

   **B.** Reaction

   **C.** Reactant

   **D.** Chemical

3. The name of the substance left after the reaction is:

   **A.** Product

   **B.** Reaction

   **C.** Reactant

   **D.** Chemical

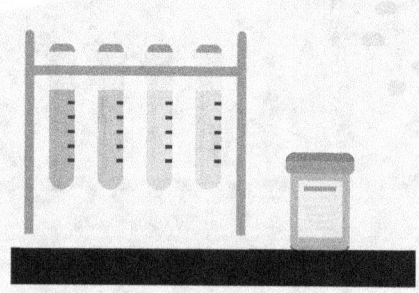

*Yesterday, you learned about how different chemicals react. Today, you will explore how these concepts work.*

**Directions:** Read each text below. Then answer the questions that follow.

## Flame Produced

Get a match and strike it. Blow it out. **Parent supervision required!**

1. Does the match look different after it has been lit?

   **A.** Yes

   **B.** No

## Gas Produced

In a bowl, mix a tablespoon of vinegar with a tablespoon of baking soda.

2. Do the products look different from the reactants?

   **A.** Yes

   **B.** No

## Color Change

Add a few drops of food coloring to a cup of water. Add a couple of drops of bleach.

3. Do you notice a color change?

   **A.** Yes

   **B.** No

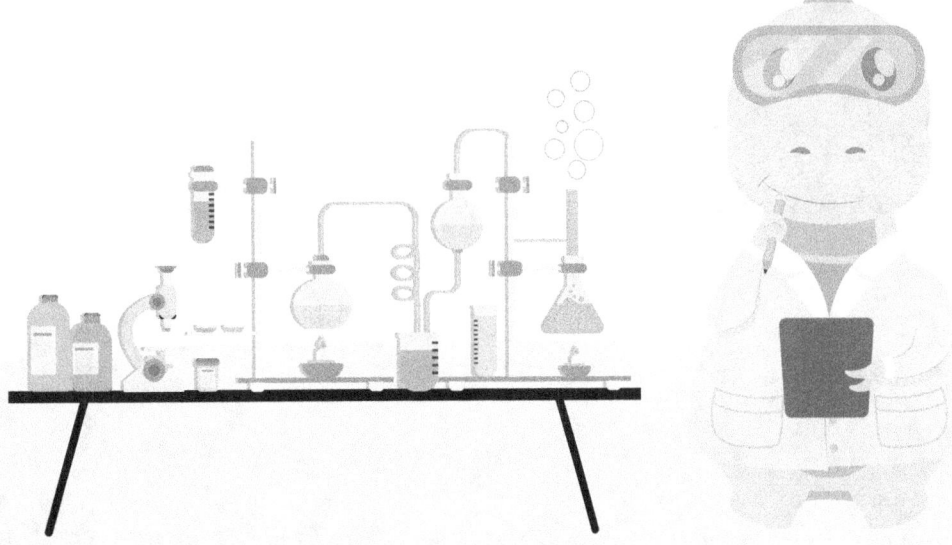

*Yesterday, you explored the concept of chemical reactions. Today, you will explain how this is possible.*

**Directions:** Read each text below. Then answer the questions that follow.

## Flame Produced

You discovered that after a match has been lit, it is different than it was beforehand.

1. Explain how lighting a match is an example of a chemical reaction.

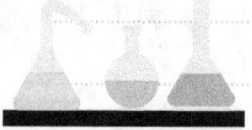

## Gas Produced

You discovered that mixing vinegar and baking soda creates gas.

2. Explain why you think mixing vinegar and baking soda is a chemical reaction.

## Color Change

You discovered that adding bleach to colored water will change its color.

3. Explain why you think mixing bleach and food coloring is a chemical reaction.

*You have spent several days learning about, exploring and explaining chemical reactions. Today, you will experiment with determining if a chemical reaction has occurred.*

### Materials:

1. Rotten fruit
2. Sparkler or small firework **(Adult Supervision Required)**
3. Paper
4. Ice

### Procedure:

1. Observe the rotten fruit. What does it look like and smell like? Record your observations.
2. Observe the sparkler or small firework. What does it look like and smell like? Record your observations.
3. Observe the paper. Rip it into pieces. What does it look like and smell like? Record your observations.
4. Observe the ice. Melt it a little. What does it look like and smell like? Record your observations.
5. Record your answers for the questions below, going back to the above items, as necessary.

### Follow-Up Questions:

1. Draw a picture of the fruit before and after it rotted.

2. Draw a picture of before and after the sparkler/firework went off.

3. Draw a picture of the paper before and after it was ripped.

4. Draw a picture of before and after the ice melted.

*Yesterday, you collected data while experimenting with chemical reactions.*

**Directions:** Read and answer each question below.

1. Were all of the four different experiments chemical reactions?

2. Which two out of the four were chemical reactions?

3. What can you conclude about chemical changes (where the actual makeup of molecules changes) versus physical changes (where a change is made but not to the molecules).

4. Chemical reactions can change the: (Select all the correct answer choices)

   **A.** shape

   **B.** size

   **C.** color

5. You know that baking is a chemical reaction. What is one sign that tells you that it is a chemical reaction?

..................................................................................................................................
..................................................................................................................................
..................................................................................................................................
..................................................................................................................................
..................................................................................................................................

6. Why do you think this?

..................................................................................................................................
..................................................................................................................................
..................................................................................................................................
..................................................................................................................................
..................................................................................................................................
..................................................................................................................................
..................................................................................................................................

# WEEK 4

# Physical Science
## Conservation of Mass

MS-PS1-5

Develop and use a model to describe how the total number of atoms does not change in a chemical reaction and thus mass is conserved.

ARGOPREP

**Directions:** Read the text below. Then answer the questions that follow.

## Mass is Conserved

When a chemical reaction takes place, the mass of all of the reactants will equal the mass of all of the products. This is called the **law of conservation of mass.** This phenomena explains that if you start with two hydrogen and one oxygen on one side of the equation, react them to get water ($H_2O$) on the other side, all of the products and the reactants will equal each other if you were to weigh them. A **chemical reaction** takes place which turns the reactants into the products. Even in a chemical reaction, **matter** is not created nor destroyed.

1. What is the term for the mass of all of the reactants equaling the mass of all of the products?

    **A.** Law of Physics

    **B.** Newton's Law

    **C.** Law of Conservation of Mass

    **D.** Law of Motion

2. What cannot be created nor destroyed?

    **A.** Atoms

    **B.** Molecules

    **C.** Elements

    **D.** Matter

3. What happens between reactants and products

    **A.** Atoms

    **B.** Molecules

    **C.** Elements

    **D.** Chemical Reactions

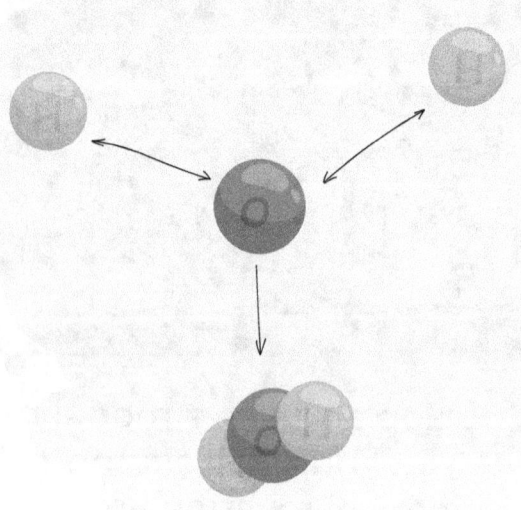

*Yesterday, you learned that mass is conserved in a chemical reaction. Today we will explore how this works.*

**Directions:** Read each text below. Then answer the questions that follow.

## Reactants

In a chemical reaction, two hydrogen and one oxygen are reacted together.

1. Do you see the two different types of atoms that are going to be reacted?

   **A.** Yes

   **B.** No

## Products

In the same chemical reaction, once reacted, we end up with water ($H_2O$) which is made of two hydrogen and one oxygen.

2. Do you notice how only one molecule is created from the atoms?

   **A.** Yes

   **B.** No

## Mass is Conserved

This equation shows that all of the single atoms that we started with are present in the products.

3. Do you notice how the atoms are rearranged to form something new?

   **A.** Yes

   **B.** No

*Yesterday, you explored the concept of conservation of mass in a chemical reaction. Today, you will explain how this is possible.*

**Directions:** Read each text below. Then answer the questions that follow.

## Atoms

You discovered the atoms that make up the reactants.

1. Explain what reactants were present in this chemical reaction.

## Elements

You discovered the atoms that make up the reactants.

2. Explain how the atoms came together to form a water molecule.

## Molecules

You discovered that the same atoms exist before and after the chemical reaction.

3. Explain how this demonstrates the law of conservation of mass.

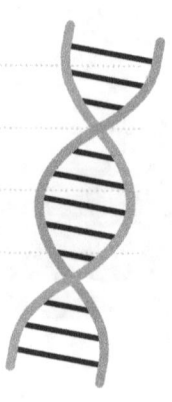

*You have spent several days learning about, exploring and explaining conservation of mass. Today, you will experiment with products and reactants.*

### Materials:

1. Kitchen scale
2. 3 plastic cups
3. white vinegar
4. heavy cream

### Procedure:

1. Fill a plastic cup about $\frac{1}{3}$ full of white vinegar.
2. Fill another plastic cup about $\frac{1}{3}$ full of heavy cream.
3. Using the kitchen scale, weigh the empty cup, the vinegar cup, and the heavy cream cup. Record this total weight.
4. Pour the heavy cream into the white vinegar. Notice the heavy cream turns into more of a solid (a sign of a chemical reaction).
5. Using the kitchen scale, reweigh the three cups and all of the liquid. Record.

### Follow-Up Questions:

1. What is the weight of all of the cups, vinegar, and heavy cream before the reaction?

........................................................................................................

........................................................................................................

........................................................................................................

2. What is the weight of all of the cups, vinegar, and heavy cream after the reaction?

........................................................................................................

........................................................................................................

........................................................................................................

3. How could you tell a chemical reaction occurred?

........................................................................................................

........................................................................................................

........................................................................................................

*Yesterday, you collected data while experimenting with a chemical reaction. Today, you will use that data to draw conclusions about how mass is conserved.*

**Directions:** Read and answer each question below.

1. What conclusion can you draw about the amount of reactants (vinegar and heavy cream) and products (liquid after the reaction)?

2. How can you prove that mass is conserved?

3. How is this similar to other chemical reactions?

4. Before and after a chemical reaction the mass of products and reactants will be:

   **A.** The Same

   **B.** Different

   **C.** Increased

5. Can you think of any other way to demonstrate this law of conservation?

.................................................................................................................................

.................................................................................................................................

.................................................................................................................................

.................................................................................................................................

.................................................................................................................................

.................................................................................................................................

.................................................................................................................................

# Physical Science

## Thermal Energy Test

MS-PS1-6

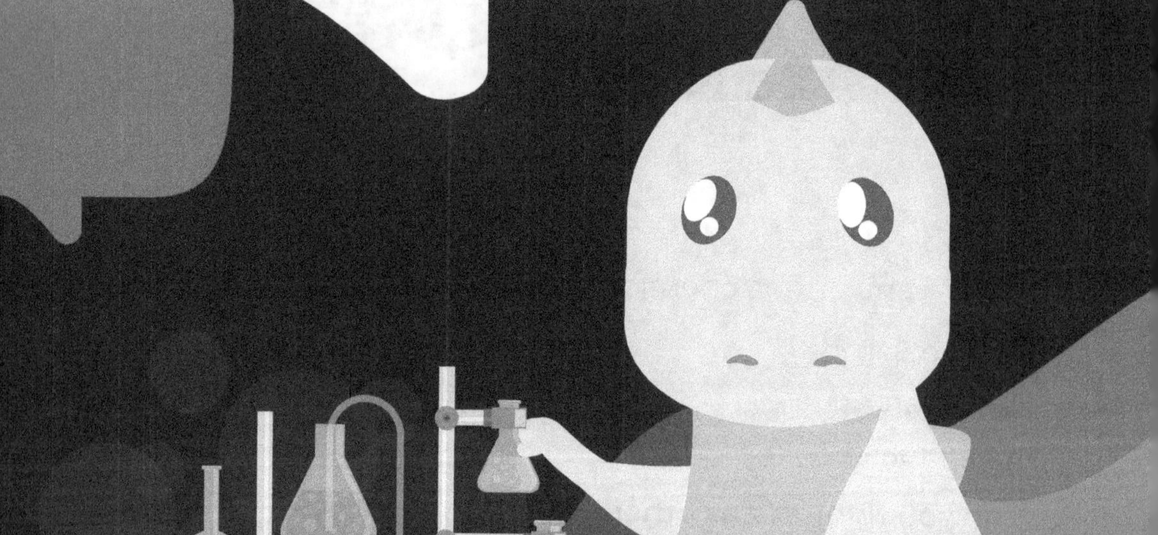

Undertake a design project to construct, test, and modify a device that releases or absorbs thermal energy by chemical processes.

**Directions:** Read the text below. Then answer the questions that follow.

## Chemical Reactions Everywhere

In some chemical reactions, thermal energy can be given off or absorbed. If thermal energy is given off, it is called an **exothermic reaction.** If thermal energy is absorbed, it is called an **endothermic reaction.** This means that in these chemical reactions, two substances combine to react and can give off OR absorb heat.

1. What is the name for a chemical reaction that gives off heat?

   **A.** Color Change

   **B.** Exothermic

   **C.** Physical Change

   **D.** Endothermic

2. What is the name for a chemical reaction that absorbs heat?

   **A.** Color Change

   **B.** Exothermic

   **C.** Physical Change

   **D.** Endothermic

3. In a chemical reaction, the term for what is produced are called the:

   **A.** Products

   **B.** Reactions

   **C.** Reactants

   **D.** Chemicals

*Yesterday, you learned there are two different types of chemical reactions that deal with heat. Today, you will explore how these concepts work.*

**Directions:** Read each text below. Then answer the questions that follow.

## Exothermic Reaction

Get a heat pack. Hit it to react the chemicals.

1. Does it get warmer to the touch?

   **A.** Yes

   **B.** No

## Endothermic Reaction

Get a cold pack from a first aid kit. Hit it to react the chemicals.

2. Does it get colder to the touch?

   **A.** Yes

   **B.** No

## Determination of Exothermic or Endothermic

Light a match. **Parent supervision required!**

3. Can you feel the heat given off by the lit match?

   **A.** Yes

   **B.** No

*Yesterday, you explored the concept of chemical reactions that give off or take in heat. Today, you will explain how this is possible.*

**Directions:** Read each text below. Then answer the questions that follow.

### Exothermic Reaction

You discovered that by mixing some chemicals inside a heat pack, heat is given off.

1. Explain how this is an example of an exothermic reaction.

### Endothermic Reaction

You discovered that by mixing some chemicals inside a cold pack, cold is given off.

2. Explain how you think this is an example of an endothermic reaction.

### Determination of Exothermic and Endothermic

You discovered that you can easily figure out if a reaction is exothermic or endothermic by the temperature.

3. Explain how you think using temperature can help to determine what kind of a reaction something is.

*You have spent several days learning about, exploring and explaining thermal energy. Today, you will experiment with chemicals that heat and cool.*

### Materials:

1. Yeast
2. Hydrogen Peroxide
3. Baking Soda
4. Vinegar
5. 2 bowls
6. Thermometer

### Procedure:

1. Place a spoonful of hydrogen peroxide into one of the bowls.
2. Using the thermometer, record the temperature of the hydrogen peroxide.
3. Add a spoonful of yeast and record the temperature again.
4. In the second bowl, pour a spoonful of vinegar.
5. Using the thermometer, record the temperature of the vinegar.
6. Add a spoonful of baking soda and record the temperature again.

### Follow-Up Questions:

1. What was the temperature of the hydrogen peroxide before the yeast was added?

.......................................................................................................

.......................................................................................................

.......................................................................................................

.......................................................................................................

.......................................................................................................

2. How much did the temperature increase or decrease when the yeast was added?

.......................................................................................................

.......................................................................................................

.......................................................................................................

.......................................................................................................

3. What was the temperature of the starting vinegar?

_____

_____

_____

_____

_____

_____

4. How much did the temperature increase or decrease when the baking soda was added?

_____

_____

_____

_____

_____

*Yesterday you collected data while experimenting with endothermic and exothermic reactions. Today, you will use that data to draw conclusions about thermal energy.*

**Directions:** Read and answer each question below.

1. Which of the two reactions represents an exothermic reaction?

2. Which of the two reactions represents an endothermic reaction?

3. What can you conclude about chemical reactions and heat?

4. A reaction that gives off heat is called:

   **A.** Endothermic

   **B.** Exothermic

   **C.** Explosive

5. You know that chemical reactions are all around us. Are there any other examples of exothermic reactions you can think of?

   ..........................................................................................................................................

   ..........................................................................................................................................

   ..........................................................................................................................................

   ..........................................................................................................................................

   ..........................................................................................................................................

6. Why do you think reactions give off heat?

   ..........................................................................................................................................

   ..........................................................................................................................................

   ..........................................................................................................................................

   ..........................................................................................................................................

   ..........................................................................................................................................

# WEEK 6

# Life Science
## Photosynthesis

MS-LS1-6

Construct a scientific explanation based on evidence for the role of photosynthesis in the cycling of matter and flow of energy into and out of organisms.

**Directions:** Read the text below. Then answer the questions that follow.

## Photosynthesis

**Photosynthesis** is the process that producers, or plants, do to use sunlight to produce sugar. Plants take in carbon dioxide (which animals breathe out), and combine it with water and sunlight. Through photosynthesis, sugar and oxygen are produced. The sugar, or glucose, is what plants use for food. It can also be consumed by animals as a food source. Primary consumers eat plants for energy, as they cannot make energy themselves.

$H_2O$

$O_2$

$O_2$

$H_2O$

SUN LIGHT

$H_2O$

$O_2$

$O_2$

$O_2$

$O_2$

$CO_2$

$CO_2$

$H_2O$

$O_2$

$O_2$

SUGAR

1. What is the term for the process that producers undergo which uses sunlight?

   A. Cellular respiration
   B. Photosynthesis
   C. Exercising
   D. Growing

2. What is NOT used for photosynthesis?

   A. Oxygen
   B. Carbon Dioxide
   C. Sunlight
   D. Water

3. What gas is produced by photosynthesis?

   A. Oxygen
   B. Carbon Dioxide
   C. Sunlight
   D. Water

*Yesterday, you learned about photosynthesis. Today we will explore how this works.*

**Directions:** Read each text below. Then answer the questions that follow.

## Inputs

Look at plants out your window. For photosynthesis to occur, they need sunlight, water, and carbon dioxide.

1. Do you see how living plants outside have access to these things?

   **A.** Yes

   **B.** No

## Outputs

Those same plants out your window are producing sugar (glucose) and oxygen.

2. Do you notice how these things can be created?

   **A.** Yes

   **B.** No

## Photosynthesis

Eat a piece of fruit. Fruit comes from plants.

3. Do you notice how sweet the fruit tastes?

   **A.** Yes

   **B.** No

# Photosynthesis

## EXPLAINING THE TOPIC

*Yesterday, you explored the concept of photosynthesis in the world around you. Today, you will explain how this is possible.*

**Directions:** Read each text below. Then answer the questions that follow.

### Inputs

You discovered the inputs (carbon dioxide, water, sunlight) required for photosynthesis.

1. Explain why these things are necessary for photosynthesis to occur.

### Outputs

You discovered the outputs created by photosynthesis.

2. Explain how the outputs are created by photosynthesis.

### Photosynthesis

You discovered the chemical reaction of photosynthesis.

3. Explain how photosynthesis demonstrates a chemical reaction.

*You have spent several days learning about, exploring and explaining photosynthesis. Today, you will experiment with seeing photosynthesis happening.*

### Materials:

1. Two clear glasses
2. Water
3. Two large leaves- spinach, romaine, etc.

### Procedure:

1. Place one large leaf in each glass.
2. Fill each glass with water.
3. Put one glass in the sunlight
4. Put one glass in a dark cupboard.
5. Wait one to two hours. Observe and record findings.
6. Answer the follow-up questions below.

### Follow-Up Questions:

1. Why do you think you put one cup in the sunlight?

.............................................................................................................................

.............................................................................................................................

.............................................................................................................................

.............................................................................................................................

.............................................................................................................................

2. Why do you think you put one cup in the dark?

.............................................................................................................................

.............................................................................................................................

.............................................................................................................................

.............................................................................................................................

.............................................................................................................................

.............................................................................................................................

**3.** Why is it important to include water in the cups?

......................................................................................................

......................................................................................................

......................................................................................................

......................................................................................................

......................................................................................................

......................................................................................................

**4.** Did anything happen after an hour?

......................................................................................................

......................................................................................................

......................................................................................................

......................................................................................................

......................................................................................................

......................................................................................................

*Yesterday, you collected data while experimenting with photosynthesis. Today, you will use that data to draw conclusions about how photosynthesis works.*

**Directions:** Read and answer each question below.

1. What did you notice about the cup in the sunlight?

2. What did you notice about the cup in the dark?

3. How does the cup in the sunlight demonstrate that photosynthesis is occurring?

4. After time in the sun, the leaf will use up some of the _____ in the process of photosynthesis.

    **A.** Water

    **B.** Food

    **C.** Soil

5. Can you think of any other way to demonstrate this phenomena?

# WEEK 7

# Life Science
## Ecosystem Resources

MS-LS2-1

Analyze and interpret data to provide evidence for the effects of resource availability on organisms and populations of organisms in an ecosystem.

ARGOPREP

**Directions:** Read the text below. Then answer the questions that follow.

## Ecosystem Resources

An **ecosystem** is made up of all the living and nonliving things in a specific area, such as a jungle or desert. In ecosystems, there are resources that plants and animals require. Plants require water, nutrients, access to sunlight, and space to grow. Animals require things such as food, water, and shelter. If the resources required to live are not avaliable, plants and animals will suffer or even die. This can affect specific organisms as well as populations of organisms within an ecosystem.

1. What is the term for all the things living organisms require?

   **A.** Resources

   **B.** Water

   **C.** Nutrients

   **D.** Shelter

2. What is NOT a requirement of plants?

   **A.** Company

   **B.** Water

   **C.** Nutrients

   **D.** Space to grow

3. What is the name for all living and nonliving things in a specific area?

   **A.** Ecosystem

   **B.** Niche

   **C.** Organism

   **D.** Resources

*Yesterday, you learned there are resources that ecosystems need. Today we will explore how this works.*

**Directions:** Read each text below. Then answer the questions that follow.

## Water as a Resource

Think about your day if you did not have access to water.

1. Would life be more difficult for you?

   **A.** Yes

   **B.** No

## Food as a Resource

Think about your day if you did not have access to food.

2. Would life be more difficult for you?

   **A.** Yes

   **B.** No

## Shelter as a Resource

Think about your day if you did not have access to shelter.

3. Would life be more difficult for you?

   **A.** Yes

   **B.** No

*Yesterday, you explored the concept of ecosystem resources in your own life. Today, you will explain how this is possible.*

**Directions:** Read each text below. Then answer the questions that follow.

## Water as a Resource

You discovered that without water, your life would look very different.

1. Explain how humans use water as a resource.

## Food as a Resource

You discovered that without food, your life would look very different.

2. Explain how humans use food as a resource.

## Shelter as a Resource

You discovered that without shelter, your life would look very different.

3. Explain how humans use shelter as a resource.

*You have spent several days learning about, exploring and explaining ecosystem resources. Today, you will experiment with resources that plants need to survive.*

### Materials:

1. Grass Seeds
2. 3 Small Cups
3. Soil
4. Water

### Procedure:

1. Put soil into the cups and plant some grass seeds. Alternatively, beans or other small seeds would work as well.
2. Wait a week or two until the plants sprout. Water every other day.
3. Then, keep one plant in the window and keep watering it, keep one plant in the window and STOP watering it, and then place one plant in a cupboard and keep watering it.
4. Compare the growth of the plants over a week's time.
5. Answer the follow-up questions.

### Follow-Up Questions:

1. Which of the ecosystem resources are you providing for the plants?

.................................................................................................................

.................................................................................................................

.................................................................................................................

.................................................................................................................

.................................................................................................................

2. What happened to the plant that had sunlight and water?

.................................................................................................................

.................................................................................................................

.................................................................................................................

.................................................................................................................

3. What happened to the plant that had water but was kept in the dark?

.......................................................................................................................

.......................................................................................................................

.......................................................................................................................

.......................................................................................................................

4. What happened to the plant that you stopped watering but still had sunlight?

.......................................................................................................................

.......................................................................................................................

.......................................................................................................................

.......................................................................................................................

*Yesterday, you collected data while experimenting with voice recordings and sound wave graphs. Today, you will use that data to draw conclusions about sound waves.*

**Directions:** Read and answer each question below.

1. Why did you put one plant in the cupboard?

..................................................................................................................

..................................................................................................................

..................................................................................................................

2. Why did you stop watering one of the plants?

..................................................................................................................

..................................................................................................................

..................................................................................................................

3. What can you conclude about the resources that plants need?

..................................................................................................................

..................................................................................................................

..................................................................................................................

4. A resource that plants need is:

   **A.** Cup to live in

   **B.** Water

   **C.** Love

5. Look out your window. How is your plant in a cup similar to a tree in the forest?

..................................................................................................................

..................................................................................................................

..................................................................................................................

6. What will happen if an organism does not have access to resources that it needs?

..................................................................................................................

..................................................................................................................

..................................................................................................................

# WEEK 8

# Life Science
## Organism Interactions

MS-LS2-1

Construct an explanation that predict patterns of interactions among organisms across multiple ecosystems.

ARGOPREP

**Directions:** Read the text below. Then answer the questions that follow.

## Ecosystem Resources

Organisms interact with each other in different ecosystems. Some of the ways that organisms interact are competition, predation, and mutually beneficial relationships. In **competition**, two organisms are competing for the same resource. For example, two different plants may be competing for water in one spot in the desert. In a **predation** situation, one predator is consuming prey, such as a lion eating a gazelle. In a **mutually beneficial** relationship, both organisms benefit. An example of this would be a remora (a fish) sticking to the side of a whale to hitch a ride around the ocean. The remora will eat some of the parasites off of the whale.

1.  What is the term for two organisms competing for the same resource?

    **A.** Competition

    **B.** Predation

    **C.** Mutually Beneficial

    **D.** Friends

2.  What is the term for one predator consuming prey?

    **A.** Competition

    **B.** Predation

    **C.** Mutually Beneficial

    **D.** Friends

3.  What is the term for an ecological relationship where both organisms benefit?

    **A.** Competition

    **B.** Predation

    **C.** Mutually Beneficial

    **D.** Friends

*Yesterday, you learned there are different ecological relationships that take place in different ecosystems. Today we will explore how this works.*

**Directions:** Read each text below. Then answer the questions that follow.

## Competition

With a friend, act out competition over a resource (a cookie for example).

1. Is it more difficult to get to the resource if you are in competition?

    **A.** Yes

    **B.** No

## Predation

With a friend, act out predation. One of you should act like a zebra and the other a lion.

2. If you were the zebra, would it be more difficult to live your life peacefully?

    **A.** Yes

    **B.** No

## Mutually Beneficial

Imagine there is a box of cookies on the top shelf of the kitchen cabinets. How could you work together to reach the cookies?

3. Is it easier to get to the food if you are getting help from someone else?

    **A.** Yes

    **B.** No

*Yesterday, you explored the concept of organism interactions in your own life. Today, you will explain how this is possible.*

**Directions:** Read each text below. Then answer the questions that follow.

## Competition

You discovered that when you are competing over a resource, it is more difficult to get to it.

1. Explain how this works in nature.

## Predation

You discovered that when a predator was attacking, it was much more difficult for the prey to go about daily life.

2. Explain how this works in nature.

## Mutually Beneficial

You discovered that when you work together with another organism, more can be accomplished.

3. Explain how this works in nature.

*You have spent several days learning about, exploring and explaining organism interactions. Today, you will gather data on organism interactions in an ecosystem.*

**Materials:**

1. Nature documentary (such as savanna, jungle, ocean)

**Procedure:**

1. Play the nature documentary.
2. Record all the examples of competition that you see.
3. Record all the examples of predation that you see.
4. Record all the examples of mutually beneficial relationships you see.

**Follow-Up Questions:**

1. How many examples of competition did you see?

2. How many examples of predation did you see?

........................................................................................................

........................................................................................................

........................................................................................................

........................................................................................................

........................................................................................................

3. How many examples of mutually beneficial relationships did you see?

........................................................................................................

........................................................................................................

........................................................................................................

........................................................................................................

........................................................................................................

4. In your opinion, which ecological relationship is the most important?

........................................................................................................

........................................................................................................

........................................................................................................

........................................................................................................

........................................................................................................

*Yesterday, you collected data while experimenting with voice recordings and sound wave graphs. Today, you will use that data to draw conclusions about sound waves.*

**Directions:** Read and answer each question below.

1. Why is competition so important in an ecosystem?

2. Why is predation important in an ecosystem?

3. Why is a mutually beneficial relationship important in an ecosystem?

4. Look out your window. Do any of these exist in the ecosystem that you live in?

**5.** How does predation keep some populations from growing to the point where animals run out of food?

.................................................................................................................................

.................................................................................................................................

.................................................................................................................................

.................................................................................................................................

.................................................................................................................................

**6.** How does competition help the stronger animals to survive?

.................................................................................................................................

.................................................................................................................................

.................................................................................................................................

.................................................................................................................................

.................................................................................................................................

# WEEK 9

# Life Science

## Cycling of Matter

MS-LS2-3

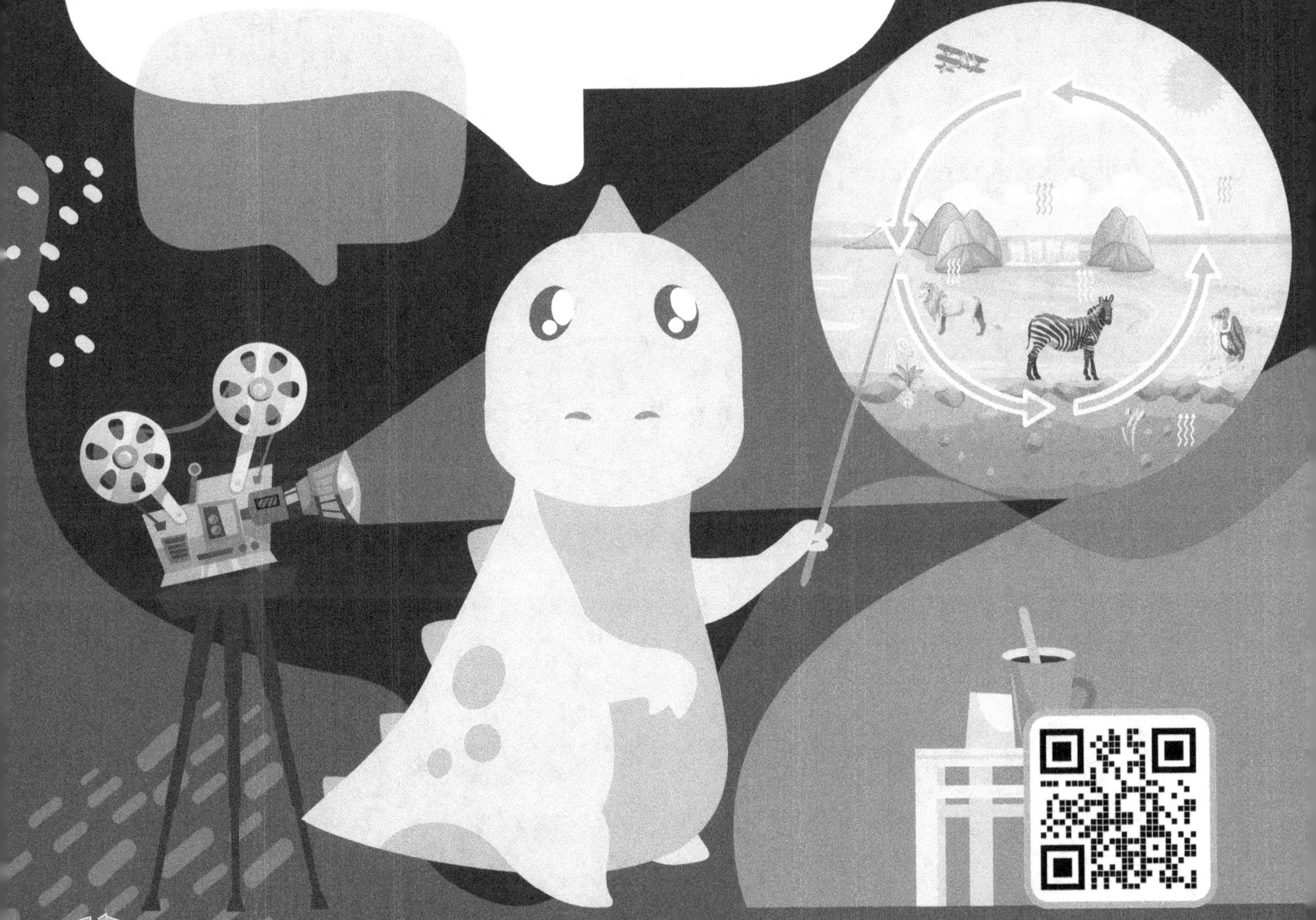

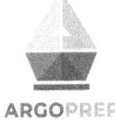

Develop a model to describe the cycling of matter and flow energy among living and nonliving parts of an ecosystem.

**Directions:** Read the text below. Then answer the questions that follow.

## Cycling of Matter

All energy comes from the sun. It gives plants solar energy so they can make sugar through a process called **photosynthesis**. Plants are called **producers** as they are the first link in the food chain, and they can produce sugar. Those plants are then eaten by animals, such as a zebra. The zebra is the **primary consumer**, as it is the first animal to eat a primary producer. A bigger animal such as a lion then eats that zebra. The lion is the **secondary consumer**, as it eats the primary consumer. When the lion dies, **scavengers** feed on the corpse. Then, **decomposers** such as bacteria or fungi break down the remains of the lion and return the nutrients (carbon, nitrogen, etc.) back to the environment. The plants can then use those nutrients to grow again.

1. What is the term for the process plants use to make sugar?

    **A.** Photosynthesis

    **B.** Decomposer

    **C.** Primary consumer

    **D.** Secondary consumer

2. What is the term for the first animal that eats a primary producer?

    **A.** Primary producer

    **B.** Primary consumer

    **C.** Decomposer

    **D.** Secondary consumer

3. What is the term for an animal that eats a primary consumer?

    **A.** Primary producer

    **B.** Primary consumer

    **C.** Decomposer

    **D.** Secondary consumer

## Cycling of Matter
### EXPLORING THE TOPIC

*Yesterday, you learned how energy comes from the sun and travels through plants and animals in an ecosystem. Today we will explore how this works.*

**Directions:** Read each text below. Then answer the questions that follow.

## Producers

Look up close at a green leaf of a plant. If it's in the winter, look at a piece of lettuce or spinach out of your refrigerator.

1. Do you notice the shape of the leaf is flat and broad?

   **A.** Yes

   **B.** No

## Primary Consumer

Eat a vegetable or piece of fruit.

2. Do you feel it is important for humans to eat plants such as fruits and vegetables?

   **A.** Yes

   **B.** No

## Secondary Consumer

Eat a piece of meat, such as chicken or beef.

3. Do you feel it is important for humans to eat animals such as chicken or beef?

   **A.** Yes

   **B.** No

*Yesterday, you explore the concept of how matter cycles through an ecosystem.*

**Directions:** Read each text below. Then answer the questions that follow.

## Producers

You discovered that plant leaves are wide and broad, to help collect sunlight.

1. Explain why it is important for plants to absorb sunlight.

## Primary Consumers

You discovered that when you consume fruits and vegetables, you are a primary consumer.

2. Explain why eating vegetables makes you a primary consumer.

## Secondary Consumers

You discovered that when you consume animals, you are a secondary consumer.

3. Explain why eating animals makes you a secondary consumer.

*You have spent several days learning about, exploring and explaining how matter moves through ecosystems.*

### Materials:

1.  Nature documentary (such as savanna, jungle, ocean)

### Procedure:

1.  Play the nature documentary.
2.  Record all the examples of producers that you see.
3.  Record all the examples of primary consumers that you see.
4.  Record all the examples of secondary consumers you see.

### Follow-Up Questions:

1.  How many examples of producers did you see?

.................................................................................................................................

.................................................................................................................................

.................................................................................................................................

.................................................................................................................................

.................................................................................................................................

2. How many examples of primary consumers did you see?

..................................................................................................................

..................................................................................................................

..................................................................................................................

..................................................................................................................

3. How many examples of secondary consumers did you see?

..................................................................................................................

..................................................................................................................

..................................................................................................................

..................................................................................................................

4. In your opinion, which of the three different ecological levels of energy moving through ecosystems (starting with producers, moving to primary consumers, then to secondary consumers) is most important?

..................................................................................................................

..................................................................................................................

..................................................................................................................

..................................................................................................................

..................................................................................................................

..................................................................................................................

*Yesterday you collected data while watching a nature documentary on producers and consumers. Today, you will use that data to draw conclusions about ecosystems.*

**Directions:** Read and answer each question below.

1. Why are producers so important in an ecosystem?

2. Why are primary consumers important in an ecosystem?

3. Why are secondary consumers important in an ecosystem?

4. Look out your window. Do any of these exist in the ecosystem that you live in?

...........................................................................................................

...........................................................................................................

...........................................................................................................

...........................................................................................................

5. How does energy get from the sun all the way to humans? Think about the things you consume.

...........................................................................................................

...........................................................................................................

...........................................................................................................

...........................................................................................................

6. How does energy get decomposed after something dies? Hint: Look back at the reading from day 1.

...........................................................................................................

...........................................................................................................

...........................................................................................................

...........................................................................................................

...........................................................................................................

...........................................................................................................

...........................................................................................................

...........................................................................................................

...........................................................................................................

...........................................................................................................

# WEEK 10

## Life Science
### Population Changes

MS-LS2-4

$CO_2$

$2x + 3y = y$

$3y = y + z$

Construct an argument supported by empirical evidence that changes to physical or biological components of an ecosystem affect populations.

**Directions:** Read the text below. Then answer the questions that follow.

## Population Changes

Populations of organisms change based on different biological and physical factors in the environment. For example, **biological factors** could include a family of deer that will increase if there are enough plants for them to eat, but decrease if the population of wolves that eat them increases. **Physical factors** that may affect the deer would be the size of the island they live on or amount of water available to drink.

1. What is the term for things such as plants and predators affecting a population?

   A. Physical Factors
   B. Biological Factors
   C. Populations
   D. Primary Consumers

2. What is the term for the size of the land and water availability affecting a population?

   A. Physical Factors
   B. Biological Factors
   C. Populations
   D. Primary Consumers

3. What is NOT one way a population is affected?

   A. Amount of water available
   B. Amount of food available
   C. Number of waterfalls
   D. Amount of predators

*Yesterday, you learned how different physical and biological factors can affect a population. Today we will explore how this works.*

**Directions:** Read each text below. Then answer the questions that follow.

## Physical Factors

Look around at the people around you.

1. Do you notice the physical environment affecting how people live?

    **A.** Yes

    **B.** No

## Biological Factors

Look at the people around you during a meal.

2. Do you notice how food availability brings people to a certain location?

    **A.** Yes

    **B.** No

## Population Changes

Think about how different types of people live around the globe.

3. Do you notice how people are adapted to live in certain areas?

    **A.** Yes

    **B.** No

*Yesterday, you explored the concept of physical and biological factors affecting ecosystems. Today you will explain further.*

**Directions:** Read each text below. Then answer the questions that follow.

## Physical Factors

You discovered the physical environment affects where people live.

1. Explain why people live in certain areas and not others.

## Biological Factors

You discovered that biological factors affect populations.

2. Explain how biological factors such as plants and animals affect where people live.

## Population Changes

You discovered that people are adapted to live in certain areas.

3. Explain why people are adapted to these areas.

*You have spent several days learning about, exploring and explaining how biological and physical factors affect ecosystems.*

**Materials:**

1. Computer for research

**Procedure:**

1. Using the computer, research people in different habitats.
2. Record how people live on mountaintops.
3. Record how people live in fishing communities.
4. Record how people live in desert communities.
5. Answer the follow-up questions on the next page.

**Follow-Up Questions:**

1. How do people on mountaintops live?

..................................................................................................................
..................................................................................................................
..................................................................................................................
..................................................................................................................
..................................................................................................................

2. How do people in fishing communities live?

..................................................................................................................
..................................................................................................................
..................................................................................................................
..................................................................................................................
..................................................................................................................

3. How do people in desert communities live?

..................................................................................................................
..................................................................................................................
..................................................................................................................
..................................................................................................................

4. Where do you live? Why do you live there?

..................................................................................................................
..................................................................................................................
..................................................................................................................
..................................................................................................................

*Yesterday, you collected data on populations of humans in different locations. Today, you will use that data to draw conclusions about populations.*

**Directions:** Read and answer each question below.

1. What biological factors affect a mountain top population?

..................................................................................................................................

..................................................................................................................................

..................................................................................................................................

..................................................................................................................................

2. What physical factors affect a mountaintop population?

..................................................................................................................................

..................................................................................................................................

..................................................................................................................................

..................................................................................................................................

..................................................................................................................................

3. What biological factors affect a fishing population?

4. What physical factors affect a fishing population?

5. What biological factors affect a desert community?

6. What physical factors affect a desert community?

7. What helps a population determine where to live?

# WEEK 11

## Life Science
## Maintaining Biodiversity

MS-LS2-5

Evaluate competing design solutions for maintaining biodiversity and ecosystem services.

ARGOPREP

**Directions:** Read the text below. Then answer the questions that follow.

## Biodiversity is Important

**Biodiversity** is what we call all of the different organisms that live in a specific area. Biodiversity is important in an ecosystem for many reasons. Having an ecosystem with a range of different organisms is better for preventing diseases from spreading, maintaining nutrients in the soil, and maintaining the overall health and stability of the ecosystem. Ecosystems are also more stable when there is a wide range of plants and animals that live in that area.

1. What is the term for the different organisms that live in a specific area?

   **A.** Biodiversity          **C.** Science

   **B.** Ecology               **D.** Chemistry

2. Which is NOT a benefit from biodiversity?

   **A.** Less disease spread          **C.** Maintenance of overall health

   **B.** Better long term stability    **D.** More expensive to maintain

3. What is the best combination for an area to thrive?

   **A.** Wide range of plants and animals

   **B.** Lots of plants, few animals

   **C.** Lots of animals, few plants

   **D.** Few animals and few plants.

*Yesterday, you learned that biodiversity is important in different ecosystems. Today we will explore how this works.*

**Directions:** Read each text below. Then answer the questions that follow.

## Plants

Go outside and walk through the woods. Observe the kinds of plants you see.

1. Do you see different kinds of plants?

   **A.** Yes

   **B.** No

## Animals

Go outside and walk through the woods. Observe the kinds of animals you see.

2. Do you notice different kinds of animals?

   **A.** Yes

   **B.** No

## Working together

Look for examples of plants and animals benefiting from each other.

3. Do you notice any examples of plants and animals benefiting from each other?

   **A.** Yes

   **B.** No

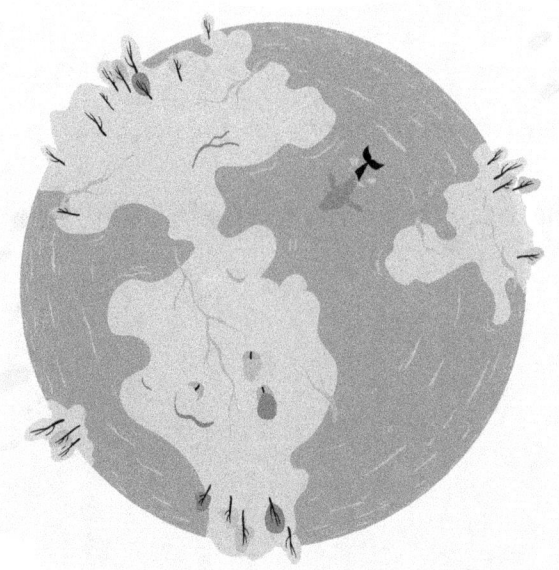

*Yesterday, you explored the concept of biological diversity. Today, you will explain how this is possible.*

**Directions:** Read each text below. Then answer the questions that follow.

## Plants

You discovered the environment is made up of many types of plants.

1. Explain why it is better to have many types of plants rather than just one.

## Animals

You discovered the environment is made up of many types of animals.

2. Explain why it is better to have many types of animals rather than just one.

## Working Together

You discovered that plants and animals work together in different ecosystems.

3. Explain how this adds to the stability of the ecosystem.

*You have spent several days learning about, exploring and explaining biodiversity in an ecosystem. Today, you will experiment with how this is possible.*

### Materials:

1. 9 Cards of a single type of tree
2. 9 Cards of multiple different types of trees

### Procedure:

1. Cut out all cards.
2. Lay out all 9 of the cards of a single type of tree with the blank side facing up. Put an X on the back of one card. The X represents a disease that only that kind of tree can get.
3. Then, put an X on the back of all the other cards that one touches that are the same kind of tree. That shows the passage of disease from one tree to another of the same species.
4. Lay out all 9 cards of the multiple types of trees with the blank side facing up. Put an X on the back of one card. The X represents a disease that only one kind of tree can get.
5. Then, put an X on the back of all the other cards that one touches that are the same kind of tree. That shows the passage of disease from one tree to another of the same type of species

### Follow-Up Questions:

1. What happened when all of the trees were the same kind?

.......................................................................................................................................

.......................................................................................................................................

.......................................................................................................................................

.......................................................................................................................................

2. What happened when all of the trees were different?

.......................................................................................................................................

.......................................................................................................................................

.......................................................................................................................................

.......................................................................................................................................

3. How are diseases passed from one organism to another?

.................................................................................................................

.................................................................................................................

.................................................................................................................

.................................................................................................................

.................................................................................................................

4. What conclusion can you draw about biodiversity?

.................................................................................................................

.................................................................................................................

.................................................................................................................

.................................................................................................................

.................................................................................................................

*Yesterday, you collected data while experimenting with biodiversity. Today, you will use that data to draw conclusions about how different organisms are better for the ecosystem.*

**Directions:** Read and answer each question below.

1. What conclusion can you draw about biodiversity?

2. Other than preventing disease transmission, why is it important to have a variety of plants and animals?

3. How does this relate to your own ecosystem?

4. What does this activity say about large factory farms that only grow one species of plant or animal?

5. Can you think of any other way to demonstrate this phenomena?

# WEEK 12

## Earth & Space Science

### Geologic Timescale

MS-ESS1-4

Construct a scientific explanation based on evidence from rock strata for how long the geologic time scale is used to organize Earth's 4.6-billion-year-old history.

ARGOPREP

**Directions:** Read the text below. Then answer the questions that follow.

## Geologic Timescale

The earth formed 4.5 billion years ago and is divided into different geologic time periods based on the organisms present at the time. This is called the **geologic timescale.** Scientists determine the age of rocks using radioactive carbon dating, which looks at the amount of carbon left in a rock over time. Another way scientists determine the age of rocks is by the **law of superposition,** which states that oldest rocks are on the bottom. Finally, scientists use **index fossils,** which are significant fossils such as seashells or trilobites found throughout history to help determine the age of rocks.

1. What is the term for the geological record of different time periods?

   **A.** Law of Superposition

   **B.** Index Fossils

   **C.** Geologic Timescale

   **D.** Earth Science

2. Which is the term for the oldest rocks being on the bottom?

   **A.** Law of Superposition

   **B.** Index Fossils

   **C.** Geologic Timescale

   **D.** Earth Science

3. What is the term for a fossil used to determine geologic age of rocks?

   **A.** Law of Superposition

   **B.** Index Fossils

   **C.** Geologic Timescale

   **D.** Earth Science

*Yesterday, you learned about the geologic timescale. Today we will explore how this works.*

**Directions:** Read each text below. Then answer the questions that follow.

## Road Cuts

Take a ride in the car on the highway. Look at the road cuts where the road goes through a hillside.

1. Do you notice different layers of rocks?

   **A.** Yes

   **B.** No

## Digging Deeper

Looking at the road cuts, observing that the oldest rocks formed at the bottom, and the newest layer is at the top- similar to sand settling over and over again on the bottom of a lake or snow falling over and over again on a mountain.

2. Do you notice the newest rocks are near the top of the hill?

   **A.** Yes

   **B.** No

## Looking for Fossils

Can you see any fossils in the rocks? Fossils are formed as layers of mud and sediment cover plants and animals and then solidify.

3. Do you notice how the rock formed one layer at a time?

   **A.** Yes

   **B.** No

*Yesterday, you explored the concept of rock layering in the geologic timescale. Today, you will explain how this is possible.*

**Directions:** Read each text below. Then answer the questions that follow.

## Road Cuts

You discovered how layers of rocks are visible through cuts in hills to make way for roads.

1.  Explain why seeing layering in rock helps support the idea of a geologic timescale.

## Digging Deeper

You discovered the top layer is the newest and the bottom is the oldest.

2.  Explain how the law of superposition relates to the road cuts.

## Looking for Fossils

You discovered that fossils could exist in these layers of rock.

3.  Explain where you would look for the oldest fossils and where you would look for the newest fossils.

*You have spent several days learning about, exploring and explaining rock layering supporting the geologic timescale. Today, you will experiment with how this is possible.*

### Materials:

1. Two bowls
2. 3 different colors of playdough
3. Four or six small objects to represent "fossils"
4. A friend to help

### Procedure:

1. You and your friend each simultaneously create your fossil setup.
2. Each of you has three colors of playdough and two to three objects.
3. Bury your objects as you layer the three colors of playdough. Record the order of your own objects, and your friend should do the same.
4. Swap bowls with your friend.
5. Excavate the fossils and try to determine which fossil was buried first.
6. Discuss with your friend and answer the follow-up questions.

### Follow-Up Questions:

1. What do the layers tell you?

..............................................................................................................................................

..............................................................................................................................................

..............................................................................................................................................

..............................................................................................................................................

2. Were you able to determine the order the fossils were buried?

..............................................................................................................................................

..............................................................................................................................................

..............................................................................................................................................

..............................................................................................................................................

3. How is this similar to road cuts?

........................................................................................................

........................................................................................................

........................................................................................................

........................................................................................................

........................................................................................................

4. How does knowing the order rocks were laid down help to determine the age of fossils?

........................................................................................................

........................................................................................................

........................................................................................................

........................................................................................................

........................................................................................................

*Yesterday, you collected data while experimenting with fossil layering. Today, you will use that data to draw conclusions about the geologic timescale.*

**Directions:** Read and answer each question below.

1. What conclusion can you draw about fossil layering?

.......................................................................................................................................

.......................................................................................................................................

.......................................................................................................................................

.......................................................................................................................................

.......................................................................................................................................

.......................................................................................................................................

2. What is the name of the law that helped you to determine the order the fossils were laid down?

.......................................................................................................................................

.......................................................................................................................................

.......................................................................................................................................

.......................................................................................................................................

.......................................................................................................................................

.......................................................................................................................................

3. How can you use the law of superposition to determine relative age of rocks?

.......................................................................................................................................

.......................................................................................................................................

.......................................................................................................................................

.......................................................................................................................................

.......................................................................................................................................

.......................................................................................................................................

**4.** What does this activity say about the history of the Earth?

_____

_____

_____

_____

_____

_____

**5.** Can you think of any other way to demonstrate this phenomena?

_____

_____

_____

_____

_____

_____

_____

# WEEK 13

# Earth & Space Science

## Geoscience Processes

MS-ESS2-2

Construct an explanation based on evidence for how geoscience processes have changed Earth's surface at varying time and spatial scales.

ARGOPREP

**Directions:** Read the text below. Then answer the questions that follow.

## Evidence of Geoscience Processes

The study of Earth science, or the processes that shape the earth, are called geoscience. Some of the processes that affect the surface of the Earth are erosion, deposition, and weathering. **Erosion** is the gradual wearing away of the surface of the Earth by wind, water, and other natural processes. **Deposition** is the geologic process where soil and rocks are added to a landform or land mass. **Weathering** is the process where rock is worn down, broken, and dissolved away into smaller and smaller pieces. All of these processes shape the surface of the earth.

1. What is the term for the gradual wearing away of the surface of the earth?

   **A.** Erosion

   **B.** Deposition

   **C.** Weathering

   **D.** Earth Science

2. Which is the term for the geologic process of soil and rocks being added to a landform?

   **A.** Erosion

   **B.** Deposition

   **C.** Weathering

   **D.** Earth Science

3. What is the term for when rocks are broken down and dissolved?

   **A.** Erosion

   **B.** Deposition

   **C.** Weathering

   **D.** Earth Science

*Yesterday, you learned about geoscience processes that shape the surface of the earth. Today we will explore how this works.*

**Directions:** Read each text below. Then answer the questions that follow.

## Erosion

Go for a ride in the car and look for examples of erosion.

1. Do you see any examples of erosion?

   **A.** Yes

   **B.** No

## Deposition

Go for a ride in the car and look for examples of deposition.

2. Do you notice any examples of deposition?

   **A.** Yes

   **B.** No

## Weathering

Go for a ride in the car and look for examples of weathering.

3. Do you notice any examples of weathering?

   **A.** Yes

   **B.** No

*Yesterday, you explored the concept of geoscience processes that affect the surface of the Earth. . Today, you will explain how this is possible.*

**Directions:** Read each text below. Then answer the questions that follow.

## Erosion

You discovered how erosion shows evidence of gradual wearing away of the surface of the Earth.

1. Explain how what you saw demonstrates erosion.

## Deposition

You discovered that deposition is the gradual addition of rocks and material to the surface of the Earth.

2. Explain how what you saw demonstrates deposition.

## Weathering

You discovered that weathering is the wearing away of material through wind and water.

3. Explain how what you saw demonstrates weathering.

*You have spent several days learning about, exploring and explaining geoscience processes that affect the surface of the Earth. Today, you will experiment with how this is possible.*

### Materials:

1. A cookie sheet or other flat pan.
2. Sand
3. Water

### Procedure:

1. Pour the sand into the flat pan.
2. Add water.
3. For geoscience process number 1, create a mountain of sand. Using drops of water, erode away some of the sand.
4. For geoscience process number 2, flatten out the sand. Push some of it to the side to create a folded mountain.
5. For geoscience process number 3, wash away the mountain using some of the water.

**Follow-Up Questions:**

1. What three geoscience processes did you demonstrate?

_____

_____

_____

_____

_____

2. What did geoscience process number 1 demonstrate?

_____

_____

_____

_____

_____

3. What did geoscience process number 2 demonstrate?

_____

_____

_____

4. What did geoscience process number 3 demonstrate?

_____

_____

_____

_____

*Yesterday, you collected data while experimenting with geoscience processes. Today, you will use that data to draw conclusions about the surface of the Earth.*

**Directions:** Read and answer each question below.

1. What conclusion can you draw about the surface of the Earth?

........................................................................................................

........................................................................................................

........................................................................................................

........................................................................................................

........................................................................................................

2. How do erosion, deposition, and weathering shape Earth's features?

........................................................................................................

........................................................................................................

........................................................................................................

........................................................................................................

........................................................................................................

3. How does deposition contribute to the formation of land features?

........................................................................................................

........................................................................................................

........................................................................................................

........................................................................................................

........................................................................................................

4. How does erosion contribute to the formation of land features?

........................................................................................................................................

........................................................................................................................................

........................................................................................................................................

........................................................................................................................................

........................................................................................................................................

5. How does weathering contribute to the formation of land features?

........................................................................................................................................

........................................................................................................................................

........................................................................................................................................

........................................................................................................................................

........................................................................................................................................

# WEEK 14

# Earth & Space Science

## Plate Tectonics

MS-ESS2-3

Analyze and interpret data on the distribution of fossils and rocks, continental shapes, and seafloor structures to provide evidence of the past plate motions.

ARGOPREP

**Directions:** Read the text below. Then answer the questions that follow.

## Evidence of Geoscience Processes

The surface of the earth is like a puzzle, with the outer layer, or the crust, of the earth broken up into different plates. These plates move due to uneven heating and cooling of material in the mantle, a layer of magma underneath the crust of the Earth. When these plates slide past each other (one moves up and one moves down for example) there is a **transform boundary.** When two plates move toward each other and crash into each other, a **convergent boundary** is formed. When two plates move away from each other to create a space between them, a **divergent boundary** is formed.

1. What is the term when two plates slide past each other?

   **A.** Transform boundary

   **B.** Convergent boundary

   **C.** Divergent boundary

   **D.** Country boundary

2. Which is the term for two plates colliding?

   **A.** Transform boundary

   **B.** Convergent boundary

   **C.** Divergent boundary

   **D.** Country boundary

3. What is the term for two plates moving away from each other?

   **A.** Transform boundary

   **B.** Convergent boundary

   **C.** Divergent boundary

   **D.** Country boundary

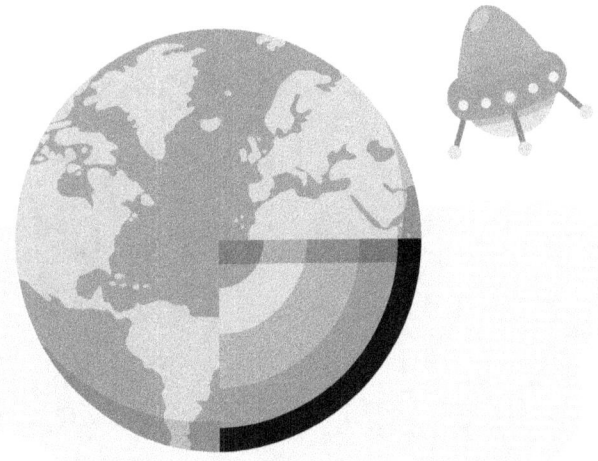

*Yesterday, you learned about plate tectonics that shape the surface of the earth. Today we will explore how this works.*

**Directions:** Read each text below. Then answer the questions that follow.

## Transform Boundary

At a transform boundary, a lot of earthquakes occur as the plates slide past each other. California has a lot of earthquakes as it is on a transform boundary.

1. Do you notice the connection between earthquakes and transform boundaries?

   **A.** Yes

   **B.** No

## Convergent Boundary

At a convergent boundary, plates pushing together create mountains like the Himilayan Mountains in India.

2. Do you notice how land colliding could create a buildup of rock, forming mountains?

   **A.** Yes

   **B.** No

## Divergent Boundary

At a divergent boundary, a valley is formed between the two plates that move apart from each other. An example of this is the mid-ocean ridge in the middle of the Atlantic Ocean.

3. Do you notice how moving materials away can create a space between the plates?

   **A.** Yes

   **B.** No

*Yesterday, you explored the concept of plate tectonics that affect the surface of the Earth. Today, you will explain how this is possible.*

**Directions:** Read each text below. Then answer the questions that follow.

## Transform Boundary

You discovered how transform boundaries create Earthquakes.

1. Explain what happens at a transform boundary.

## Convergent Boundary

You discovered that convergent boundaries create mountains.

2. Explain what happens at a convergent boundary.

## Divergent Boundary

You discovered that divergent boundaries create valleys between mountains.

3. Explain what happens at a divergent boundary.

*You have spent several days learning about, exploring and explaining plate tectonics that affect the surface of the Earth. Today, you will experiment with how this is possible.*

### Materials:

1. Graham Crackers
2. Frosting
3. Plate

### Procedure:

1. Spread some frosting onto the plate.

2. Break up the graham crackers
3. Using the graham crackers as plates, demonstrate a transform boundary.
4. Using the graham crackers as plates, demonstrate a convergent boundary.
5. Using the graham crackers as plates, demonstrate a divergent boundary.
6. Answer the follow-up questions.

### Follow-Up Questions:

1. What three plate tectonic processes did you demonstrate?

..................................................................................................................................

..................................................................................................................................

2. How did you demonstrate a transform boundary?

..................................................................................................................................

..................................................................................................................................

3. How did you demonstrate a convergent boundary?

..................................................................................................................................

..................................................................................................................................

4. How did you demonstrate a divergent boundary?

..................................................................................................................................

..................................................................................................................................

*Yesterday, you collected data while experimenting with geoscience processes. Today, you will use that data to draw conclusions about the surface of the Earth.*

**Directions:** Read and answer each question below.

1. What conclusion can you draw about the plates on the surface of the Earth?

2. How do the different types of plate boundaries shape Earth's features?

3. What occurs at a transform boundary?

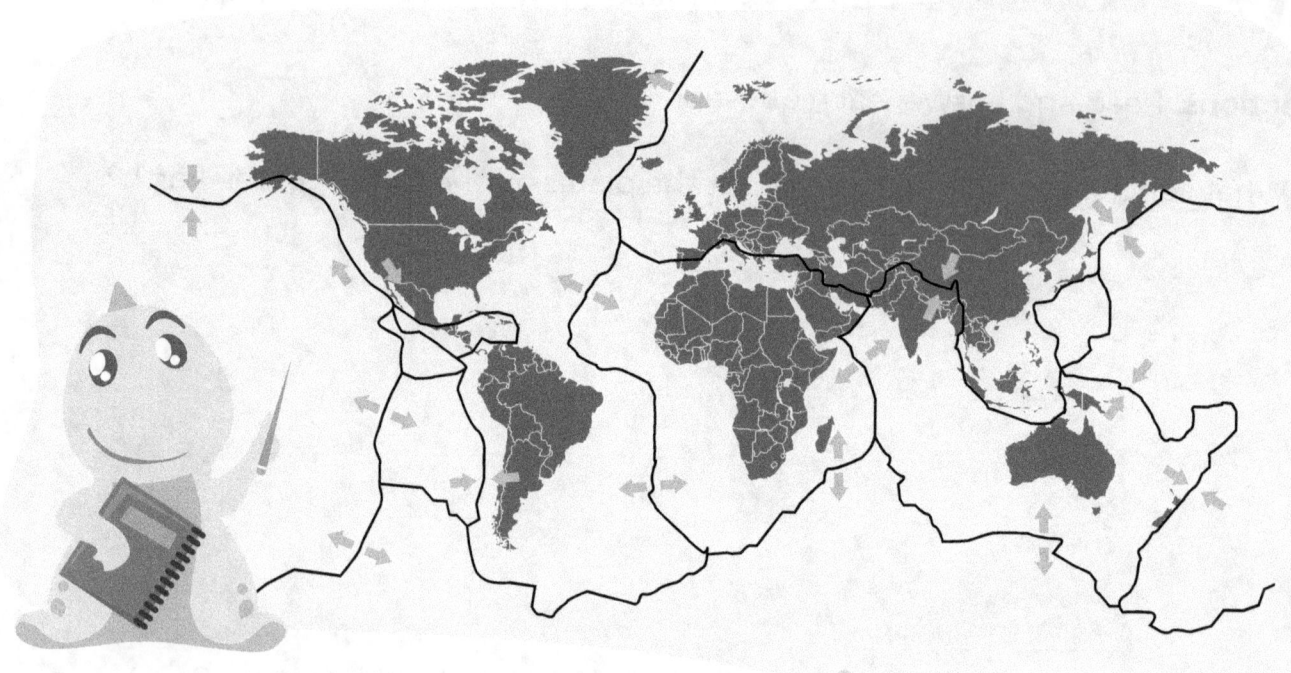

**4.** What occurs at a convergent boundary?

..................................................................................................................................................

..................................................................................................................................................

..................................................................................................................................................

..................................................................................................................................................

..................................................................................................................................................

**5.** What occurs at a divergent boundary?

..................................................................................................................................................

..................................................................................................................................................

..................................................................................................................................................

..................................................................................................................................................

..................................................................................................................................................

# WEEK 15

# Earth & Space Science

## Cycling of Earth's Materials

MS-ESS2-1

Develop a model to describe the cycling of Earth's materials and the flow of energy that drives this process.

ARGOPREP

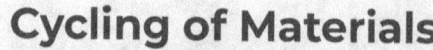
**Directions:** Read the text below. Then answer the questions that follow.

## Cycling of Materials

Materials such as rocks, minerals, and water move around the surface of the earth in predictable cycles. Rocks melt as they are pulled down into the Earth's crust (outer layer) and **mantle** (level under the crust). Some melted rocks form **crystals,** which are made of minerals and they grow in pockets in the Earth's crust. Weathering is the process that breaks down materials using wind and water, and sedimentation is the building up of materials over time. Rocks can move through these phases and the **rock cycle** continues.

1. What is the term for rocks moving through different phases?

   **A.** Crystals

   **B.** Melted Rock

   **C.** Rock Cycle

   **D.** Earth's Crust

2. Which is the term for minerals that grow in pockets in the Earth's crust?

   **A.** Crystals

   **B.** Melted Rock

   **C.** Rock Cycle

   **D.** Earth's Crust

3. What is the term for the layer under the Earth's crust?

   **A.** Crystals

   **B.** Mantle

   **C.** Rock Cycle

   **D.** Earth's Crust

*Yesterday, you learned about how materials cycle through the Earth. Today we will explore how this works.*

**Directions:** Read each text below. Then answer the questions that follow.

## Mantle

Make a slurry of cornstarch and water. This is the texture of the material in the mantle.

1. Do you notice the way this material is easy to deform and move around?

   **A.** Yes

   **B.** No

## Crystals

Pour out some salt or sugar. These are crystals.

2. Do you notice how crystals are small shapes of minerals?

   **A.** Yes

   **B.** No

## Rock Cycle

Take a starburst and melt it in your hand. Put it in the freezer to solidify again.

3. Do you notice how materials can melt and reharden?

   **A.** Yes

   **B.** No

*Yesterday, you explored the concept of the rock cycle. Today, you will explain how this is possible.*

**Directions:** Read each text below. Then answer the questions that follow.

## Mantle

You discovered how the mantle is made up of semi-liquid rock.

1. Explain how the semi-liquid material of the mantle allows the Earth's crust to move around on top of it.

## Crystals

You discovered that familiar materials like salt and sugar are made up of crystals.

2. Explain how crystals are different from other rocks.

## Rock Cycle

You discovered that rocks can be melted and hardened again.

3. Explain what happens in the rock cycle.

*You have spent several days learning about, exploring and explaining the rock cycle. Today, you will experiment with how this is possible.*

### Materials:

1. Boiling water
2. Jar
3. Popsicle stick
4. String
5. Sugar
6. Stove
7. Pan

### Procedure:

1. Dissolve 2 cups of sugar in 1 cup of water over the stove.
2. Pour sugar/water mixture into a jar.
3. Tie the string to the popsicle stick.
4. Hang the string into the water.
5. Wait a few days until sugar crystals form on the string.
6. You have formed sugar crystals, also known as rock candy.
7. Answer the follow-up questions.

### Follow-Up Questions:

1. What did you create?

_____

_____

2. What did you have to do to the sugar to get it to harden into crystals?

_____

_____

3. Why did you heat the water?

_____

_____

4. Could this be recreated with salt? Explain.

_____

_____

*Yesterday, you collected data while experimenting with the rock cycle. Today, you will use that data to draw conclusions about the cycling of Earth's materials.*

**Directions:** Read and answer each question below.

1. What conclusion can you draw about the formation of crystals?

2. What would happen if you tried to make rock candy without heating the sugar crystals up?

3. How are crystals similar to other rocks?

4. How are crystals different from other rocks?

........................................................................................................................

........................................................................................................................

........................................................................................................................

........................................................................................................................

........................................................................................................................

5. Explain how the rock candy could be melted down and the rock cycle you have created could continue.

........................................................................................................................

........................................................................................................................

........................................................................................................................

........................................................................................................................

........................................................................................................................

# WEEK 16

# Earth & Space Science

## Cycling of Water

MS-ESS2-4

Develop a model to describe the cycling of water through Earth's systems driven by energy from the sun and the force of gravity.

ARGOPREP

**Directions:** Read the text below. Then answer the questions that follow.

## Water Cycle

The water cycle is the Earth's way of moving water through solid, liquid, and gas phases. Water exists in the liquid phase in oceans, rivers, and streams. It exists in the gas phase as water vapor, and it exists in the solid phase as snow and ice. **Evaporation** is when water moves up to clouds as water vapor, **condensation** is when it collects in clouds, and **precipitation** is when water comes out of clouds as rain and snow.

1. What is the term for water moving up toward the clouds?

   **A.** Condensation

   **B.** Precipitation

   **C.** Evaporation

   **D.** Ice

2. Which is the term for water collecting in clouds?

   **A.** Condensation

   **B.** Precipitation

   **C.** Evaporation

   **D.** Ice

3. What is the term for water coming out of clouds as rain or snow?

   **A.** Condensation

   **B.** Precipitation

   **C.** Evaporation

   **D.** Ice

*Yesterday, you learned about how water cycles through different phases. Today we will explore how this works.*

**Directions:** Read each text below. Then answer the questions that follow.

## Evaporation

Pour a glass of water and leave it in the sun.

1. Do you notice how over time the water leaves the glass?

   **A.** Yes

   **B.** No

## Condensation

Boil some water in a pot with a lid. **Parent supervision required!**

2. Do you notice how steam condenses on the lid of the pot?

   **A.** Yes

   **B.** No

## Precipitation

Go outside when it rains, hails, or snows.

3. Do you notice how water comes down out of the clouds?

   **A.** Yes

   **B.** No

*Yesterday, you explored the concept of the water cycle that affects the different states of water. Today, you will explain how this is possible.*

**Directions:** Read each text below. Then answer the questions that follow.

## Evaporation

You discovered how evaporation is possible with little more than the sun.

1. Explain how evaporation works.

## Condensation

You discovered that water vapor can collect and form droplets.

2. Explain how condensation works.

## Precipitation

You discovered that precipitation can take many different forms.

3. Explain where precipitation comes from.

*You have spent several days learning about, exploring and explaining the water cycle. Today, you will experiment with how this is possible.*

**Materials:**

1. Sandwich bag
2. Water
3. Permanent Marker
4. Masking Tape

**Procedure:**

1. Pour $\frac{1}{4}$ of a cup of water into the sandwich bag and seal it up.
2. Tape it up into a sunny window.
3. Wait a few hours.
4. Where the water is at the bottom, write "reservoir."
5. Where the foggy part at the top of the bag is, write "condensation."
6. Where the water runs down the sides of the bag, write "precipitation."
7. Over the water, write "evaporation."
8. You have created the water cycle inside of a sandwich bag!
9. Answer the follow-up questions.

**Follow-Up Questions:**

1. What did you create?

......................................................................................................................

......................................................................................................................

......................................................................................................................

......................................................................................................................

......................................................................................................................

2. What is driving the water cycle that you created?

......................................................................................................................

......................................................................................................................

......................................................................................................................

......................................................................................................................

......................................................................................................................

3. What was the purpose of heating the water?

....................................................................................................
....................................................................................................
....................................................................................................
....................................................................................................

4. Where is the water coming from that condenses at the top of the bag?

....................................................................................................
....................................................................................................
....................................................................................................
....................................................................................................

*Yesterday, you collected data while experimenting with the water cycle. Today, you will use that data to draw conclusions about the cycling of water on Earth.*

**Directions:** Read and answer each question below.

1. What conclusion can you draw about the cycling of water?

2. How is this sandwich bag model similar to the water cycle on Earth?

3. How is this sandwich bag model different to the water cycle on Earth?

4. What would happen to your model if there was no heat from the sun powering it?

5. Can you think of any other way to demonstrate the water cycle phenomena?

# WEEK 17

# Earth & Space Science

## Earth's Resources

MS-ESS3-1

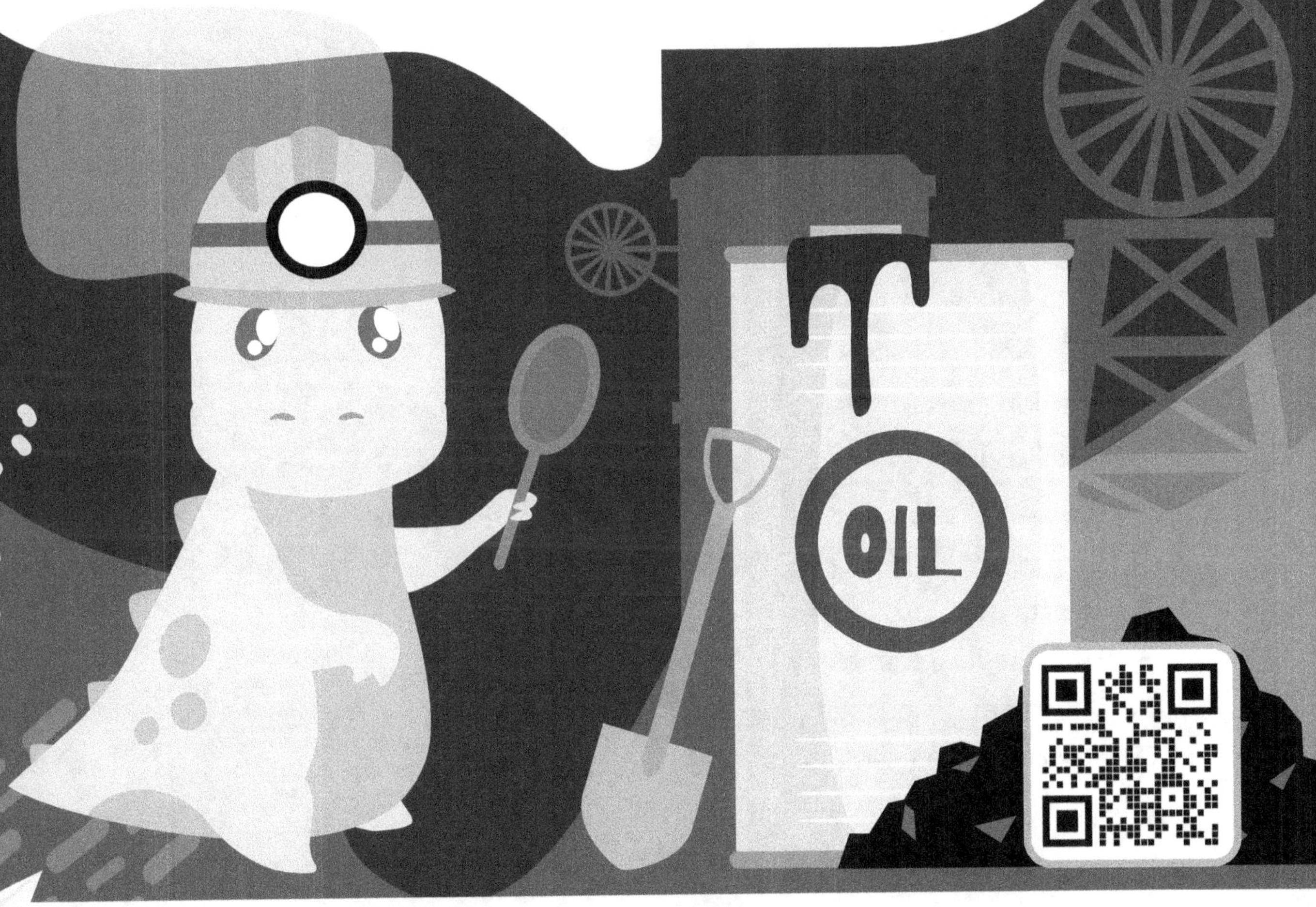

Construct a scientific explanation based on evidence for how the uneven distributions of Earth's mineral, energy, and groundwater resources are the result of past and current geoscience processes.

**Directions:** Read the text below. Then answer the questions that follow.

## Earth's Resources

Resources are not distributed around the Earth evenly. There are pockets of different materials in different places. Earth's minerals, energy, and groundwater resources are the result of past and current geoscience processes, such as plate tectonics, the rock cycle, the water cycle, and the formation of fossil fuels from decaying organic (once living) material. Oil, coal, and gas are our fossil fuels that are made out of dead organisms from millions of years ago.

1. Which of the following is NOT a fossil fuel?

   A. Oil

   B. Coal

   C. Gas

   D. Groundwater

2. How are resources distributed around the Earth?

   A. Evenly

   B. Unevenly

   C. The same everywhere

   D. In a single layer

3. What is the term for plate tectonics, the rock cycle, the water cycle, and the formation of fossil fuels?

   A. Geoscience processes

   B. Biological processes

   C. Chemical processes

   D. Physical processes

*Yesterday, you learned about how Earth's resources are not distributed evenly. Today we will explore how this works.*

**Directions:** Read each text below. Then answer the questions that follow.

## Minerals

Research where you find salt on the Earth.

1. Do you notice how it is not distributed evenly?

   **A.** Yes

   **B.** No

## Groundwater

Research where you find fresh water on the Earth.

2. Do you notice how it is not distributed evenly?

   **A.** Yes

   **B.** No

## Fossil Fuels

Research where you find fossil fuels on the Earth.

3. Do you notice how they are not distributed evenly?

   **A.** Yes

   **B.** No

*Yesterday, you explored the concept of Earth's resources being unevenly distributed. Today, you will explain how this is possible.*

**Directions:** Read each text below. Then answer the questions that follow.

## Minerals

You discovered how minerals are unevenly distributed.

1. Explain why minerals are important for humans (salt for example).

## Groundwater

You discovered that groundwater is unevenly distributed.

2. Explain why having a supply of fresh water is important for humans.

## Fossil Fuels

You discovered that fossil fuels are unevenly distributed.

3. Explain where fossil fuels come from.

*You have spent several days learning about, exploring and explaining the uneven distribution of Earth's resources. Today, you will experiment with how fossil fuels are hard to collect.*

### Materials:

1. Drinking glasses (2)
2. Water
3. Vegetable Oil
4. Coffee Filter
5. Assorted spoons, straws, etc.

### Procedure:

1. Fill the first glass $\frac{1}{4}$ of the way with oil.

2. Fill the remaining $\frac{3}{4}$ of the first glass with water.

3. Using the coffee filter and tools, try to separate the oil from the water. Place it in the second glass.

### Follow-Up Questions:

1. What are you separating?

.......................................................................................................................

.......................................................................................................................

2. How is vegetable oil like crude oil?

.......................................................................................................................

.......................................................................................................................

3. What tools were effective to separate the two liquids?

.......................................................................................................................

.......................................................................................................................

4. How is this different from oil engineers working in the field?

.......................................................................................................................

.......................................................................................................................

*Yesterday, you collected data while experimenting with Earth's resources, particularly fossil fuels in the form of oil. Today, you will use that data to draw conclusions about the resources on Earth.*

**Directions:** Read and answer each question below.

1. How was yesterday's activity similar to oil engineers working in the field?

2. Why is it important to be able to collect and use Earth's resources?

3. What is different between collecting a non-renewable resource such as oil than collecting a renewable resource such as water?

4. Why is it important to conserve non-renewable resources such as oil?

_____

_____

_____

_____

_____

5. Can you think of any other non-renewable resources?

_____

_____

_____

_____

_____

# WEEK 18

# Earth & Space Science

## Natural Hazards

MS-ESS3-2

Analyze and interpret data on natural hazards to forecast future catastrophic events and inform the development of technologies to mitigate their effects.

ARGOPREP

**Directions:** Read the text below. Then answer the questions that follow.

## Forecasting Natural Hazards

Natural hazards occur all over the Earth. Some hazards are more likely to occur in some areas than others. For example, **tsunamis** are more likely to happen in the Pacific Ocean as they are caused by an underwater earthquake that creates a wave that travels a far distance before it hits land. The Pacific Ocean is the largest ocean on the Earth, so it has a far distance for the waves to travel. Furthermore, there are many islands susceptible to wave damage due to having low elevation above sea level. **Volcanoes** are more likely to occur on plate boundaries, such as the Pacific Ring of Fire. **Earthquakes** are most likely to occur at transform boundaries. **Hurricanes** and **tornadoes** are also natural hazards, and technology is getting better and better at predicting these catastrophic events.

1. What is the term for an event caused by an underwater earthquake that generates a big wave?

   **A.** Tsunami

   **B.** Earthquake

   **C.** Hurricane

   **D.** Tornado

2. Where on Earth are there most likely volcanoes?

   **A.** Colorado

   **B.** Pacific Ring of Fire

   **C.** Atlantic Ring of Fire

   **D.** Canada

3. What of the following is NOT a natural hazard?

   **A.** Volcano

   **B.** Earthquake

   **C.** Power Outage

   **D.** Tsunami

*Yesterday, you learned about how natural hazards affect the Earth. Today we will explore how these work.*

**Directions:** Read each text below. Then answer the questions that follow.

## Volcano

Research where you can find the most volcanoes occuring.

1. Do you notice how they are not distributed evenly on the Earth?

   **A.** Yes

   **B.** No

## Earthquake

Research where you can find the most earthquakes occurring.

2. Do you notice how they are more common in some places than others?

   **A.** Yes

   **B.** No

## Tsunami

Research where you find the most tsunamis occuring.

3. Do you notice how they are more common in some places than others?

   **A.** Yes

   **B.** No

*Yesterday, you explored the concept of natural hazards being unevenly distributed. Today, you will explain how this is possible.*

**Directions:** Read each text below. Then answer the questions that follow.

## Volcano

You discovered how volcanoes are unevenly distributed.

1. Explain why being able to predict volcanic eruptions is important.

## Earthquake

You discovered that earthquakes are unevenly distributed.

2. Explain why being able to predict earthquakes is important.

## Tsunami

You discovered that tsunamis are unevenly distributed.

3. Explain why being able to predict tsunamis is important.

*You have spent several days learning about, exploring and explaining the uneven distribution of natural hazards around the Earth. Today, you will experiment with volcanoes specifically.*

## Materials:

1. Tray
2. Vinegar
3. Baking soda
4. Small soda bottle
5. Newspaper
6. Glue
7. Water
8. Paint (optional)

## Procedure:

1. Stand up the soda bottle on a tray.
2. Rip the newspaper into strips. Using watered-down glue as paper mache', build the shape of a volcano around the outside of the soda bottle.
3. Let your volcano dry and paint it if desired.
4. Go outside.
5. Put some baking soda in the soda bottle.
6. Add vinegar and watch the explosion!
7. Answer the follow-up questions.

## Follow-Up Questions:

1. What did you create?

........................................................................................

........................................................................................

........................................................................................

2. What happened when you added baking soda and vinegar?

........................................................................................

........................................................................................

........................................................................................

**3.** How is this similar to real volcanoes?

....................................................................................................................

....................................................................................................................

....................................................................................................................

....................................................................................................................

**4.** How is this different from real volcanoes?

....................................................................................................................

....................................................................................................................

....................................................................................................................

....................................................................................................................

....................................................................................................................

*Yesterday, you collected data while experimenting with a model of a volcano. Today, you will use that data to draw conclusions about the hazards on Earth.*

**Directions:** Read and answer each question below.

1. How was yesterday's activity similar to the lava flow of real volcanoes?

2. Would it be safe to have your volcano explode like real volcanoes?

3. Why should humans be aware of natural hazards?

4. If you are afraid of natural hazards, are there places you should choose to live and places you should choose to avoid?

5. Can you think of a way to demonstrate any other natural hazard?

# Earth & Space Science

## Human Impact

MS-ESS3-3

Apply scientific principles to design a method for monitoring and minimizing a human impact on the environment.

ARGOPREP

**Directions:** Read the text below. Then answer the questions that follow.

## Human Impact on the Environment

With **7.8 billion** people on the Earth, humans have a staggering impact on the environment. Humans burn fossil fuels, are responsible for deforestation, and pollute rivers and waterways. Humans also contribute to trash buildup worldwide, which ends up in places such as the **Great Pacific Garbage Patch,** which is a huge garbage patch made up mostly of plastic. While the human impacts on the environment sound terrible, there are steps you can take to reduce your negative impact on the environment.

1. How many people are on the Earth?

   **A.** 7.8 billion
   **B.** 8.7 billion
   **C.** 7.8 million
   **D.** 500 million

2. What is the name of the location where there is plastic built up in the ocean?

   **A.** Great Pacific Garbage Patch
   **B.** Great Atlantic Garbage Patch
   **C.** Great Southern Ocean Garbage Patch
   **D.** Great Arctic Ocean Garbage Patch

3. What is NOT a negative impact that humans have on the environment?

   **A.** Garbage building up
   **B.** Deforestation
   **C.** Pollution
   **D.** Planting Gardens

*Yesterday, you learned that humans are having a huge negative impact on the planet. Today we will explore how this works.*

**Directions:** Read each text below. Then answer the questions that follow.

## Burning Fossil Fuels

We burn fossil fuels such as coal, gasoline, oil, and natural gas. Look around your life and see where your family uses these things.

1. Do you see that you use fossil fuels for things like heat and to power cars?

   **A.** Yes

   **B.** No

## Deforestation

Humans cut down trees for things like paper products, cardboard, and furniture. Look around and count how many products you can find that are made of paper or wood.

2. Do you notice how paper products are everywhere?

   **A.** Yes

   **B.** No

## Trash Buildup

Collect your trash for a single day.

3. Does the amount of trash you generate in a single day surprise you?

   **A.** Yes

   **B.** No

*Yesterday, you explored the concept of how humans impact their environment. Today, you will explain how this is possible.*

**Directions:** Read each text below. Then answer the questions that follow.

## Burning Fossil Fuels

You discovered that humans burn fossil fuels.

1. Explain what humans use fossil fuels for.

## Deforestation

You discovered that humans cut down forests for many purposes.

2. Explain what humans use wood products for.

## Trash Buildup

You discovered that humans generate a lot of trash.

3. Explain where all of that trash goes.

*You have spent several days learning about, exploring and explaining human impact on the environment. Today, you will experiment with reducing your impact.*

### Materials:

1. All of the trash you use in a single day.
2. Trash bag
3. Scale
4. Recycling Bin
5. Trash Bin
6. Compost Bin

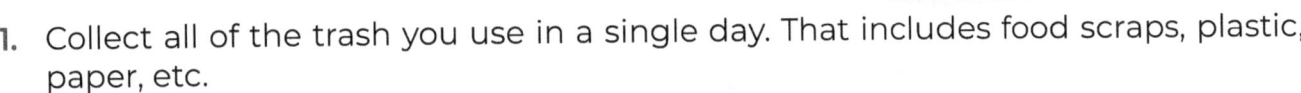

### Procedure:

1. Collect all of the trash you use in a single day. That includes food scraps, plastic, paper, etc.
2. Weigh all of the trash.
3. Split it up into things you can compost (such as vegetable scraps, coffee, eggshells, etc.).
4. Split it up into things you can recycle (such as paper, clean plastic, cardboard, etc.
5. Put the remainder into the trash. Weigh this amount again.
6. Answer the follow-up questions.

### Follow-Up Questions:

1. What is the weight of all of your trash?

........................................................................................................................................

........................................................................................................................................

2. What is the weight of all of your trash after you take out the recyclables and compost?

........................................................................................................................................

........................................................................................................................................

3. How could you reduce your trash further?

........................................................................................................................................

........................................................................................................................................

*Yesterday, you collected data while experimenting with a chemical reaction. Today, you will use that data to draw conclusions about how mass is conserved.*

**Directions:** Read and answer each question below.

1. What conclusion can you draw about the amount of trash you generate in a single day?

2. What could you do in order to ensure more of what you use is compostable?

3. How can you use more recyclable products?

4. Where do recycled items end up?

...........................................................................................

...........................................................................................

...........................................................................................

...........................................................................................

...........................................................................................

5. Where does trash end up?

...........................................................................................

...........................................................................................

...........................................................................................

...........................................................................................

...........................................................................................

# WEEK 20

# Earth & Space Science

## Human Populations

MS-ESS3-4

Construct an argument supported by evidence for how increases in human population and per-capita consumption of natural resources impact Earth's systems.

**Directions:** Read the text below. Then answer the questions that follow.

## Human Population Growth

The population of humans on Earth is almost at 7.8 billion! Each human has basic needs, such as food, water, and shelter. Think about the resources that you use in a single day. Think about the amount of food you eat, the water you drink, and the amount of trash that you generate. As the human population continues to increase, the per-capita consumption of natural resources are negatively impacting Earth's systems.

1. What of the following is NOT impacted by human population?

   A. Amount of water used

   B. Amount of trash generated

   C. Amount of food consumed

   D. Amount of sunshine available

2. What is not something consumed by humans?

   A. Plants

   B. Animals

   C. Trash

   D. Water

3. Which of the following is NOT a basic need of humans?

   A. Water

   B. Food

   C. Shelter

   D. Electricity

*Yesterday, you learned that the human population is impacting the resources on the Earth. Today we will explore how this works.*

**Directions:** Read each text below. Then answer the questions that follow.

## Food

Go to the grocery store and observe people at the checkout station.

1. Do you notice families purchasing more groceries than individuals?

   **A.** Yes

   **B.** No

## Shelter

Do some research on different types of human shelters.

2. Do you notice how all humans need some type of shelter?

   **A.** Yes

   **B.** No

## Trash

Do some research on the average amount of trash people in your country produce.

3. Do you notice how some people create more trash than others?

   **A.** Yes

   **B.** No

*Yesterday, you explored the concept of humans using resources from the Earth. Today, you will explain how this is possible.*

**Directions:** Read each text below. Then answer the questions that follow.

## Food

You discovered that humans consume a lot of food.

1. Explain why it is so important for humans to have food every single day.

## Shelter

You discovered that humans create all types of shelters.

2. Explain why it is so important for humans to have shelter every single day.

## Trash

You discovered that humans generate trash everyday.

3. Explain how it is possible for humans to generate so much trash.

*You have spent several days learning about, exploring and explaining how the human population affects the Earth. Today, you will experiment with water usage.*

### Materials:

1. Water
2. Your daily life
3. Computer for research

### Procedure:

1. Go about your normal day but record every single time you use water. Don't forget things like laundry, washing dishes, watering plants, etc.
2. Try to calculate how much water you use in a single day.
3. You may need to use your computer to get an estimate (of how much water a washing machine uses, for example).
4. Answer the follow-up questions.

**Follow-Up Questions:**

1. What is the total amount of water you use in a day?

2. Is this amount more or less than other humans in your country?

3. What did you do that used the most water?

4. What did you do that used the least amount of water?

*Yesterday you collected data on the amount of water you use in a single day. Today, you will use that data to draw conclusions about resource use.*

**Directions:** Read and answer each question below.

1. What conclusion can you draw about the amount of water the total population of the world will use?

2. How can you conserve water?

3. Are there other resources you could conserve?

4. Why is it important to use our resources wisely?

................................................................................................................

................................................................................................................

................................................................................................................

................................................................................................................

................................................................................................................

5. Water is a renewable resource. Why is this a good thing?

................................................................................................................

................................................................................................................

................................................................................................................

................................................................................................................

................................................................................................................

# Answer Sheets

To see the answer key to the entire workbook, you can easily download the answer key from our website!

*Due to the high request from parents and teachers, we have removed the answer key from the workbook so you do not need to rip out the answer key while students work on the workbook.

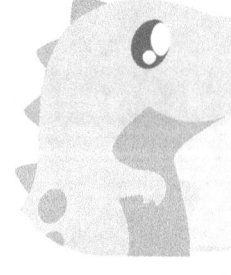

To watch free video explanations go to: **argoprep.com/science7**
OR scan the QR Code:

**Place your mouse over the workbook you have, and you will see the "Download Answers" button.**

**For detailed video instructions on how to access the "Answer Sheets," please scan this QR code.**

6th Grade Science: Daily Practice Workbook | 20 Weeks of Fun

3rd Grade Science: Daily Practice Workbook | 20 Weeks of Fun...

4th Grade Science: Daily Practice Workbook | 20 Weeks of Fun...

7th Grade Science: Daily Practice Workbook | 20 Weeks of Fun...

5th Grade Science: Daily Practice Workbook | 20 Weeks of Fun...

8th Grade Science: Daily Practice Workbook | 20 Weeks of Fun...

Kindergarten Science: Daily Practice Workbook | 20 Weeks of Fun...

1st Grade Science: Daily Practice Workbook | 20 Weeks of Fun...

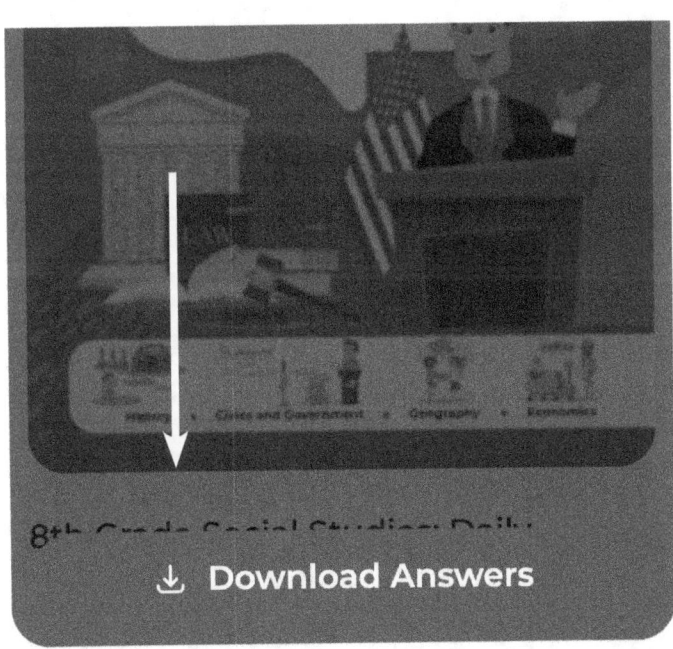

8th Grade Social Studies: Daily

⤓ Download Answers

4th Grade Social Studies: Practice Workbook

www.ingramcontent.com/pod-product-compliance
Lightning Source LLC
Chambersburg PA
CBHW081329120626
46546CB00011B/3276